DEVOTION TO THE NINE CHOIRS OF HOLY ANGELS,

AND ESPECIALLY TO THE ANGEL-GUARDIANS.

TRANSLATED FROM THE FRENCH OF

HENRI-MARIE BOUDON,
ARCHDEACON OF EVREUX.

BY.
EDWARD HEALY THOMPSON, M.A.

"Nonne omnes sunt administratorii spiritus, in ministerium missi propter eos qui hæreditatem capient salutis?"—*Htb*. i, 14.

london:
BURNS, OATES, & CO.,
17 & 18 portman street, portman square;
and 63 paternoster row.
dublin: kelly, 8 grafton street. 1869

PRINTED BY BALLANTYNE AND COMPANY EDINBURGH AND LONDON

CONTENTS

ADVERTISEMENT. 1
    PART I. Motives for this Devotion................................5
    PART II. Practice of this Demotion 11

DEVOTION TO THE NINE CHOIRS OF ANGELS. ....2̲
    PART I. Motives for this Devotion.............................33
    PART II. Practice of this Devotion..........................105

A PRAYER TO THE NINE CHOIRS OF HOLY ANGELS. 172
POSTSCRIPT..17̲4
LITANY OF THE HOLY ANGELS..176
A PRAYER TO ALL ANGELS 181
LITANY OF OUR HOLY ANGEL-GUARDIAN......................18̲2
TRANSLATOR'S NOTES 185

i

ADVERTISEMENT

THIS translation of what may, perhaps, be called the most popular of all Boudon's works, was undertaken with the desire of furthering the holy object for which it was written, in the way which the venerable author specially recommended; for one of the means, and, indeed, one of the chief means, which he prescribes for spreading devotion to the Holy Angels, is the distribution of well-selected books on the subject. "This means," he writes, "includes almost all the others, since it both gives them honour and teaches it."

In the absence of any treatise on the due mode of honouring these blessed spirits, it is hoped that the present publication may be found a Useful contribution to our devotional literature. Such a treatise, it is believed, has long been felt to be a desideratum among English-speaking Catholics; and that Boudon's work was well adapted to supply the want, may be inferred from the fact, that several persons of piety and judgment were desirous of having it translated, and that more than one had actually entered on the task before they were aware that the present performance was completed and ready for press.

The popularity which this little book has attained, and has continued to retain, in France, is sufficient evidence of its intrinsic merits; and, indeed, it would not be easy to produce a work equal to it in simplicity, unction, and power. It is superfluous to add that the doctrines it contains are not the offspring of the writer's imagination, or his mere private opinions, but that they rest on the solid basis of Catholic theology, and are in faithful accordance with the teaching of the Church.

In his zeal for the honour of God, the author has been led to descant at some length on the irreverence, indifference, and penuriousness of which men are guilty in regard to the Blessed Sacrament of the Altar. All this may appear irrelevant to the subject of which he is treating, but, not to mention that it springs naturally from the consideration that angels are the guardians of churches and altars, such digressions may be taken as exemplifications of his own habitual practice of the devotion he is recommending: the thought of some scandal or abuse occurs to his mind, as he writes, and forthwith, while himself prescribing remedies, he turns, as by a natural movement of piety, to the Holy Angels for sympathy and counsel, confers with them about the matter, and implores their assistance in correcting the evil. Anyhow, it was felt to be more satisfactory, and more respectful to the saintly writer, to publish his work entire, without omission or abridgment.

Again, there are some portions of the subject which might perhaps have been more fully treated with advantage ; but others there are which this experienced master of the spiritual life may be truly said to have well-nigh exhausted. Such is the detailed description of the various solicitations, stratagems, and subtleties which the devils employ for the deterioration and destruction of souls; a description which, at least, must have the effect of showing the real practical nature of the devotion which it is the object of the book to inculcate. For if the spirits of hell are possessed of such tremendous power and craft, and are allowed to exercise both one and the other in assaults upon mankind—and what reader of the Bible can doubt the fact?—of what importance, of what unspeakable personal importance, to every one of us, it is that we should secure the aid of those far mightier beings—mightier because they are the servants and the friends of God—who are commissioned by Him to protect and assist the heirs of salvation.

In explaining the particular office which the choir of the Powers fulfils in reference to men, the author makes an observation which applies with especial force to these our times:—"When we see storms gathering either in the Church or in the State, combinations to resist those who are working for the glory of God, extraordinary conspiracies to defeat some great good which is being planned in dioceses, towns, country-districts, and provinces—then it is that we ought to perform frequent devotions in honour of these Powers of Heaven, that they may overturn and destroy all the might and miserable plottings of hell." Such combinations and extraordinary conspiracies we now see forming around and against the Church in almost every country of Europe, fostered and even avowedly organised by irreligious and infidel governments—machinations so cunningly contrived and so unrelentingly pursued, that we may well believe that they can only have their origin in Satanic hate and malice. Against these "plottings of hell" God has given to His Church the protection of His holy angels, incomparable in their love and pity for men and their zeal for the Divine interests. Mighty, therefore, as our adversaries are, and seemingly irresistible in their fury, we may by the aid of these glorious spirits baffle all their wicked counsels, and scatter their forces like chaff before the wind.

The pious author is especially urgent in recommending devotion, not only to the angelic hierarchies in the general, but to each of the nine choirs in particular. There is one way of practising this devotion which is becoming common in this country, but to which attention may here be suitably directed. It is that of honouring the Sacred Heart of Jesus in union with the nine choirs of angels by means of an association of worshippers leagued together for that holy purpose. This pious association is formed of different bands, each band consisting of nine adorers. To each of these adorers is assigned every month a distinct office of devotion, to be discharged in conjunction with one of the nine choirs of angels. Thus every associate enjoys the special assistance of all the blessed spirits in that particular choir, and is enabled to worship the Sacred Heart in a more perfect way ; his adoration also suffers less intermission, and, indeed, may be said to become perpetual, seeing that the heavenly adorers supply his place when either his necessary avocations or sleep render attention on his own part impossible.

Such persons as may desire to take part in this holy league will find full directions for forming associations and regulating the exercises of the members in a little book published by Messrs Bichardson, and entitled "Method of Honouring the Sacred Heart of Jesus, extracted from the Life of the Blessed Margaret Mary Alacoque."

E. H. T.
Cheltenham,
Michaelmas, 1869.

EXHORTATION TO LOVE AND DEVOTION FOR THE HOLY ANGELS.

It is the property of great things to be indescribable. The excellences of the angels cannot worthily be expressed. All possible motives urge us to love them. Men are moved to love by different considerations ; and all these consider¬ations oblige us to love the angels. Every kind of good is to be found in their love. Their friendship is incomparable. Their love pursues us everywhere. Yet devotion to them is rare. This is owing to the absence of the interior life. The more exalted the angels are, the greater their love and their power. The author's desire to rouse men from their inseneibilty. The world's forgetfulness of God ; and of God's angels. The language of the Fathers respecting them. The author calls upon all sorts of men to love all the nine choirs with a particular love. He invokes the blessing of God upon all who practise devotion to them... page 1

PART I.

MOTIVES FOR THIS DEVOTION.

FIRST MOTIVE.

THE ADMIRABLE PERFECTIONS OF THESE SUBLIME INTELLIGENCES.

The greatness of the angels beyond the thought of man to conceive. They are spirits pure and bright. Why they are called Intelligences. How they are represented in Scripture. Their marvellous power. Their enchanting beauty. Everything about them enrapturing. They are the mirrors of God's perfections. Called by the name of God in Scripture. .... page 33

SECOND MOTIVE.

THE INCOMPARABLE GOODNESS OF THESE SPIRITS OF LOVE.

Angels the kings of heaven. They love us with every variety of love.

Their love untiring and unchangeable. They are our best and oldest friends. Yet they meet with nothing but ingratitude and contempt from men. Hence their love for men is past understanding. ....page 38

THIRD MOTIVE.

ALL THE HOLT ANGELS ARE ENGAGED IN THE SERVICE OF MEN.

All the angels are ministering spirits ; even the highest and most exalted. Proofs of this from Scripture. Their numbers exceedingly great. What gratitude we ought to feel to these princes of heaven, and what joy and confidence in their friendship..page 41

FOURTH MOTIVE.

ALL MEN ARE ASSISTED BY THE HOLT ANGELS.

The love of God to man has no other motive but itself. The smallest sin has in it something terrible and abominable : the angels clearly discern this, yet cease not to assist sinners. Heretics and unbelievers have their protecting angels; even Antichrist will have a guardian-angel. No excess of malice and ingratitude prevents these beings of heavenly purity from devoting themselves to the service of men............ page 43

FIFTH MOTIVE.

THE HOLT ANGELS DO ALL THAT IS POSSIBLE
TO BE DONE FOR THE GOOD OF MEN.

Angels have assumed visible forms in the service of men. They accompany us everywhere, despite our folly and vileness. The princes of

Paradise are our servants and slaves. They watch over everything belonging to us. Scripture instances. The whole world is full of them. ....page 46

SIXTH MOTIVE.

THE HOLY ANGELS ASSIST US IN TEMPORAL THINGS.

Their considerate kindness and liberality. They have care of our bodily nature and sustenance ; and confer all sorts of benefits upon us. Instances of this from Scripture and the Lives of Saints. They deliver us from all kinds of evil, and assist us in all our distresses. Instance of the pillar of cloud and of fire that accompanied the people of Israel. ....page 50

SEVENTH MOTIVE.

THE HOLT ANGELS RENDER US GREAT SERVICES FOR ETERNITY.

The affair of eternity the one great affair. The zeal which the angels show to procure men the life of grace. The care they take to maintain and increase it. They instil a love of all virtues, and especially of purity. They inspire men with love for Jesus and Mary. An incident in the life of St Dominic. They communicate light to the understanding and pious impulses to the heart. They preserve from sin, and deliver from it. They animate and encourage in labours and sufferings....................page 55

EIGHTH MOTIVE.

THE PROTECTION OF THE HOLY ANGELS AGAINST THE DEVILS, WITH PARTICULAR REFERENCE TO THEIR DIFFERENT TEMPTATIONS, WHICH ARE HERE TREATED OF.

Life one long temptation. We are weak, and our enemies are mighty. The devils cruel in their rage. Their formidable setrength. Their subtle machinations. The devil ever busy in laying snares. Baits them cunningly. Attacks if he cannot seduce. Chooses well his time. Feigns to retreat. Amuses with a false peace. These wicked spirits mislead souls in the ways of grace. Turn men aside from their true vocation. Tempt them to frustrate God's intentions. Delude them in the matter of prayer, confession, and com¬munion. The artifices they employ in the highest paths of grace. They tempt to presumption, impatience, weariness, despair. Distort the imagination even of good people. Take advantage of their smallest imperfections. Present false notions of devotion. Insinuate a censorious and critical spirit. Raise persecutions against the servants of God. Promote scandals and abuses. Some persons their special instruments. The devils find their stronghold in heresy. They are indefatigable in pursuit. They penetrate everywhere. Their assaults more violent in proportion to our love of God. Their number beyond conception. Our blindness and insensibility. The power of humility and of self-mistrust. We must avoid occasions of temptations ; and be prompt in resisting. When chastity is assailed the only safety is in flight. Remedies to be adopted in case of other interior sufferings ; scruples, or other disquietudes ; temptations to blasphemy, or the idea of reprobation. Living by faith the sure rule of the spiritual life. It is one of the devil's stratagems to make us be occupied with anything but what we ought to be about. Another is to give us a taste for occupations which are not suitable to our state. Against all the artifices of hell God has given us the defence of His holy angels. Instances of their protecting power. The devils have a great dread of them.......................... page 60

NINTH MOTIVE.

THE GREAT ASSISTANCE WHICH THE HOLY ANGELS AFFORD US AT THE HOUR OF DEATH, AND AFTER DEATH.

On the moment of death hangs the sentence of eternity. The thought of God's judgments terrible. The angels our friends when creatures abandon us. Blessed are they who have been devout to them during life. The angels present our souls before the tribunal of God............page 91

TENTH MOTIVE.

DEVOTION TO THE HOLY ANGELS IS A MARK OF A HIGH PREDESTINATION.

That which passes away deserves only our contempt. The human heart is made for great things. The joys of the blessed in heaven are unequal. We ought to strive after the highest honours for the sake of the greater glory of God. Devotion to the angels contributes wonderfully to the per¬fection of divine love, and therefore to the increase of heavenly glory. The higher the angels the more of God there is in them. Our devotion rarely extends beyond those of the lowest choir.. page 94

ELEVENTH MOTIVE.

THE GLORY OF THE MOST HOLY VIRGIN.

The glory of the Blessed Mother of God a powerful motive. The zeal of the angels for the interests of their Queen. Therefore the motive of her glory is one of the most powerful in promoting devotion to the angels. The several titles which belong to her in connexion with these heavenly spirits. The angels are the "friends" of the spouse in the Canticles. .... page 97

TWELFTH MOTIVE.

GOD ONLY.

God all in all to the soul that loves with a pure love. It cares for nothing save His sacred interests ; self-interest is an abomination to it. God only forms the whole occupation of a glorious eternity. Very few love God after a perfect manner. We must love the angels only in God and for God. Illustration taken from the spouse in the Canticles. Pure love a state of universal death to everything. .... page 99

PART II.

PRACTICE OF THIS DEMOTION

FIRST PRACTICE.
TO HAVE A PARTICULAR DEVOTION TO THE ANGELS, ARCHANGELS, AND PRINCIPALITIES.

The different offices of these three orders. We ought to have a singular devotion to our Angel-Guardians. We ought also to be devout to the Guardian Angels of our friends. Among our friends our spiritual directors ought to hold a prominent place. We must honour also the angels of our benefactors, of our enemies, of the prelates of the Church, especially the Sovereign Pontiff, as also of temporal princes. The Archangels of kingdoms and provinces, of towns and villages, must be objects of our devotion. Churches and altars have their Guardian Angels. The author laments the profanations committed against the Blessed Sacrament; carelessness in giving communion ; penuriousness in pro¬viding altar furniture. He invokes the assistance of the holy angels in remedying these evils, and entreats pious souls to seek their aid. Not only dioceses, but communities and confraternities have their angels. Special virtues to be acquired through these three orders.......page 113

SECOND PRACTICE.

TO HONOUR ESPECIALLY THE POWERS, THE VIRTUES, AND THE DOMINATIONS.

The different offices of these three orders. We are apt to mis¬take our own will for the will of God. Devotion to the Dominations a great remedy to this disorder. We are easily led by our inclinations. Devotion to the Virtues our resource. The Virtues ought to be invoked in times of public calamity. To the Powers, God has given a special strength against the might and malice of the devils. Their aid to be sought to protect the Church against her enemies..page 126

THIRD PRACTICE.

TO HAVE A PROPOUND REVERENCE AND EXTRAORDINARY LOVE FOR THE THRONES, CHERUBIM, AND SERAPHIM.

The Seraphim excel in the pure love of God. Eight properties of this love. The special attribute of the Cherubim is light. The Thrones are in close vicinity to the glory of God, and repose upon Him. The peace which passeth understanding is to be sought through their ministry. The science of Heaven, which is the science of the Saints, is to be learned at the feet of Jesus Crucified through the teaching of the Cherubim. The hatred which the devils bear to directore who inculcate this science. The Seraphim are the sacred ministers of divine love. The Carmelite order destined, by their super-excellent grace, to fill the seats of the apostate spirits of this choir. ....page 130

FOURTH PRACTICE.

TO HAVE A GREAT DEVOTION TO ST MICHAEL, ST GABRIEL, ST RAPHAEL, AND THE FOUR OTHER ANGELS WHO ABE BEFORE THE THRONE OF GOD.

St Michael, the great saint of the cause of God and of God Incarnate. The meaning of the title Archangel as applied to the highest princes of Heaven. St Gabriel negotiated the mystery of the Incarnation. St Raphael, the great benefactor of men. Emblems of the seven angels. They will obtain us the seven gifts of the Holy Spirit, and grace to avoid the seven deadly sins.. page 137

FIFTH PRACTICE.

TO HOLD INTERIOR CONVERSE WITH THE HOLY ANGELS.

Our conversation ought to be heavenly ; therefore we ought to converse frequently with these spirits of Heaven. Men live in oblivion of the world of grace. Where there are numbers of people there are also numbers of angels ; yet we take no notice of them. Our neglect of our angel-guardian. We ought to converse habitually with him. We need never feel solitary. We may visit in spirit heathen and heretical lands, and converse with their angel-guardians. It is a laudable practice to salute the angels of those we meet. These practices may be unusual, but they ought to be common. ....page 142

SIXTH PRACTICE.

TO PERFORM NOVENAS IN HONOUR OF THE NINE CHOIRS OF ANGELS.

This practice an efficacious means for obtaining the assistance of Heaven in times of distress. God employ these blessed spirits to work wonders. Directions how to employ each day of the novena. Public calamities the effects of God's anger. This devotion a fitting preparation for the feasts of our Lord and His Blessed Mother. Pious exercises to be used.. page 151

SEVENTH PRACTICE.

TO TAKE CERTAIN DAYS EVERY MONTH AND EVERY WEEK FOR THE PURPOSE OF HONOURING MORE ESPECIALLY THE HOLY ANGELS, AND TO CELEBRATE THEIR FEASTS WITH ALL POSSIBLE DEVOTION.

How to dedicate every day in the week to their honour. We may make our birth-day a feast of our angel-guardian. Feasts of St Michael. Pilgrimages to his Mount in Normandy. His apparitions. Legend of his slaying the dragon. St Gaudentius : invention of his body and miracles wrought at his tomb. Feasts of St Gabriel, St Raphael, and the Guardian Angels. The rosary of our angel-guardian. How to honour the angel-guardians of the Saints. .... page 155

EIGHTH PRACTICE.

TO VISIT CHURCHES AND ORATORIES DEDICATED TO GOD IN HONOUR OF THE HOLY ANGELS.

Certain localities honoured by God with special favours. Pilgrimages approved by the Church, and highly esteemed by Saints. It is a pious practice to visit some chapel or altar dedicated to the angels. Revival of devotion to St Michael in the city of Rouen blessed by God. Visits of devotion during nine succeeding days. .... page 165

NINTH PRACTICE.

TO PLACE GREAT CONFIDENCE IN THE PROTECTION OF THE HOLY ANGELS, AND TO HAVE RECOURSE TO THEM IN ALL OUR NECESSITIES, BODILY AND SPIRITUAL.

The angels are as impregnable bulwarks to those who trust in the Lord. How great, then, ought to be our confidence. The blindness of men exemplified in the conduct of Eliseus's servant. The little confidence they place in the protection of Heaven. Revelations which Saints have had of the presence and ministrations of angels. Our Lord employed their ministry ....page 168

TENTH PRACTICE.

TO LABOUR FOR THE CONVERSION OF SOULS, AND FOR THEIR RELIEF IN THE FLAMES OF PURGATORY, IN HONOUR OF THE HOLY ANGELS.

The angels do all for the glory of God; and we ought to labour with them for the interests of God in souls. The extravagance of men where self is concerned; their niggardliness when God's interests are at stake. The example of the angels a powerful motive for succouring souls. Like them we ought to assist the souls in Purgatory. Pious practices for this end. Our forgetfulness of the dead. Revelations of the interest taken by angels in suffering souls..page 173

ELEVENTH PRACTICE.

TO PRACTISE SOME VIRTUE, OR ABSTAIN FROM SOME VICE, IN HONOUR OF THE HOLY ANGELS.

If we desire to love the angels, we must love what they love and hate what they hate. Miraculous deliverance of a young nobleman. Humility, purity, and prayer the virtues dearest to the angels. Their jealousy for the

Divine interests. Instance of this. We must be careful not to do anything to offend them. Plato's doctrine on the subject.......................page 181

TWELFTH PRACTICE.

TO PROMOTE IN ALL KINDS OF WAYS DEVOTION TO THE NINE CHOIRS OF HOLY ANGELS.

Our gratitude to these heavenly spirits ought to be as comprehensive as our duties towards them. The great thing is to have a real love. One means of honouring them is to dis¬tribute pictures of them, and books composed in their honour. The rich can erect churches, or chapels, or altars to them. Preachers ought to instruct the people in devo¬tion to them. Bishops and superiors can recommend it to pastors and flocks. Pious persons can confer together to promote it.....................page 186

CONCLUSION OF THIS LITTLE WORK BY THE PLAN OF AN ASSOCIATION IN HONOUR OF THE NINE CHOIRS OF ANGELS.

Associations instituted for various objects. The object of this association would be to hasten the reign of Jesus and Mary. The members should make a general confession. Special times for communion. Daily, monthly, and yearly observances. Other practices of piety and virtue. The associates must have a great horror of sin, and espe¬cially of impurity. In towns a solemn novena may be kept ....page 191

  A PRAYER TO THE NINE CHOIRS OF HOLY ANGELS...................... 199
  POSTSCRIPT 201
  LITANY OF THE HOLY ANGELS 202
  A PRAYER TO ALL ANGELS 204
  LITANY OF OUR HOLY ANGEL-GUARDIAN 205
  TRANSLATOR'S NOTES 207

GOD ONLY.

To Our Lady of the Angels.

Great Queen of Paradise, Sovereign Empress of those blessed spirits who enjoy an eternal repose and felicity inconceivable, prostrate at thy feet, where all that need find help, the greatest sinners a refuge, the persecuted an asylum, the afflicted consolation, the weak a support, the desolate a mighty defence ; those sacred feet, where the unbeliever finds faith, the heretic grace to submit himself to the Holy Catholic Church, the sinner conversion, the lukewarm fervour, the blind light, the feeble fortitude and strength, the just true holiness ; those glorious feet, where the most exalted souls receive the brightest illuminations of heaven, learn the purest maxims of Jesus Christ, thy Son, our God, are instructed in the most solid truths of religion, are set on fire with the burning flames of pure love, and are arrayed in a garment of perfect justice ; those dear feet of my good and faithful Mistress, where I would fain live and die—prostrate before thee, O my powerful Protectress, I offer and present to thee, I dedicate and consecrate to thee, this little work, wholly consecrated and devoted to the honour of the Nine Choirs of Angels, thy faithful subjects, and the illustrious princes of thy heavenly court. As thou art their amiable Princess, their august Empress, and glorious Lady, it is meet that I should dedicate to thy greatness that which regards their interests and their glory; and more than this, O my most holy Lady, thou knowest that I possess nothing which is not thine : this is a truth which it is sweet to me to repeat and publish aloud on all occasions, esteeming, as I do, the title of thy servant an honour beyond compare, which I desire inviolably to preserve, and which from my whole heart I prefer to all that is greatest and most glorious upon earth. Bless, O thou most holy, this little work ; bless it with thy holiest benedictions, for thou hast an interest in it, as in a thing which belongs to thee, and is all thine. Obtain for all who shall read it the unction of grace ; make it, by the power of Jesus, thy beloved Son, a means of establishing and promoting devotion to all the Choirs of the Angels for the honour and glory of God Only, our beginning and our sole end in all things. God Only, God Only, God Only.

GOD ONLY.

To my Good Angel Guardian.

My lord and faithful guide of my life, when I reflect on what thou art and what I myself am—when I think of my ingratitude and thy incredible goodness to me—my mind is, as it were, lost in an abyss. I am confounded, and am able only to say, Thou art a bright intelligence of the Blessed Eternity, a pure spirit, a spirit all light and splendour, a spirit of pure love, a great prince of the empyrean, and one of the mighty kings of Paradise ; and as for me, I am but dust and ashes, a vile lump of clay, a blind and miserable wretch, a very great sinner, yea, the worst of sinners. Here in thy holy presence I declare—I desire to say it before all men, and to publish it everywhere—that I look upon myself as deserving, not only the last place upon earth, but the lowest place in hell—below all the devils—and acknowledge myself to be the vilest creature in the whole world.

And yet thou deignest to love a creature such as this ; thou art pleased to bestow a watchful care on all that concerns it ; to assist it in all its needs, interior and exterior, to defend it against all its enemies, to support it against all the power of hell ; thou art pleased—O inconceivable thought!—to accompany it continually, to be its inseparable companion; and thou rejoicest in loading it with benefits, notwithstanding all the contempt, infidelity, and ingratitude with which it hath treated thee. Next to the love of Jesus and Mary, who ever heard of love like this? Surely it is a love unparalleled in constancy and fidelity; a love the most disinterested, the tenderest, the most patient, the most beneficent ; love the most merciful, the most generous, the strongest, the most devoted.

Great prince, why dost thou love me thus? Whence is it that there is not a single moment of my life which is not marked by some benefit of thine? O my soul, it is sweet to thee to muse upon the signal mercies for which thou art indebted to this dear prince of thy life. It is sweet to thee to remember how he hath saved thee from hell, to recollect the graces he hath obtained for thee, the unspeakable assistance he hath given thee on all occasions, the loving care he hath taken of all that regards both thy temporal and thy spiritual interests. O my lord, what return can I make thee for all these benefits? Ah! too clearly do I see that it is impossible for me to make any worthy acknowledgment for the exceeding favours thou hast shown me. Should I give thee thanks with every breath I draw, it were but a small requital. O my soul, what, then, shall we do? Let us enter into the powers of the Lord,* and offer out of the Sacred Hearts of Jesus and Mary a worthy thanksgiving for so much goodness. When we have thought and said everything, it will not be enough; should we even give our life for so beneficent a prince, we should not pay the debt we owe him, replenished as we have been through his favour with every manner of blessings, and delivered from every kind of evil

But, O most amiable prince, as both words and strength fail me, I would speak to thee through the Precious Heart of the Adorable Jesus and that of His most holy Mother. Alas! I know well that I cannot comprehend the ineffable language of those Sacred Hearts; but at least I desire to say all that They will say to thee for me. Receive as my thanksgiving, which I fain would pay thee, but cannot, the thanks that They will offer thee. Let them be for ever the just reward of thy services and the rich acknowledgment of all thy love. My heart also pledges itself by an inviolable resolution to love thee truly. O my lord, bestow, I pray thee, thy benediction on these good desires, and on the sincere intention which I have to honour thee by all the actions of my life, in God only, and for God only, desiring to live as thy servant and the servant of all the Nine Choirs of Angels for the remainder of my days. Our Blessed Lady will rejoice that her servant should be thy servant also, as well as of all the other Princes of Heaven, thy companions, and that his whole life should be devoted to honour thee and them, together with herself, unceasingly, to its last moment, and throughout eternity, and that all his days here below should be like so many festivals of Paradise.

Present, dear ruler of my heart, this resolution which thou knowest I have long taken, together with this little work, to all the Three Hierarchies, to all the Nine Angelic Choirs—the burning Seraphim, the radiant Cherubim, the glorious Thrones, the mighty Dominations, the divine Virtues, the tremendous Powers, the sacred Principalities, the holy Archangels, and the loving Angels; and say to them all which thou wilt know so well how to say in thy angelic fashion, and which I am wholly unable to express. The offering of a miserable life like mine, and of this poor work, is most unworthy of their deserts; but do thou supply my poverty and my imperfections. Coming from thy hand, an angelic hand, Angels cannot but receive it graciously. Tell them also that my heart is full of desire to honour and to love them in a far more excellent way; and that fain would it possess the hearts of all men to give them to all the angelic choirs, that they may present them without reserve to the Most Amiable Hearts of Jesus and Mary, where reigns, and ever has reigned, God Only. It is this God Only, O most faithful, most constant, and most loving of my friends, whom I desire in all these desires : but once again, O my lord, for an end so worthy, bestow thy holy blessing upon all the days of my life and at the awful hour of death. Amen. Amen. God Only, God Only, God Only—Who is the end of all devotion to the most holy Virgin, to the Angels, and the Saints, and Whom I desire to honour without ceasing in all the honours which I render them.

Note
* "Quoniam non cognovi litteraturam, introibo in potentias Domini," Ps. lxx. 15.

DEVOTION TO THE NINE CHOIRS OF ANGELS.

GOD ONLY.

Exhortation to Love and Devotion for the Holy Angels.

The knowledge of the wise, says the Holy Spirit in Ecclesiasticus, is like, in its abundance, to the overflowing of waters;[1] for even as we see fields and whole lands covered and submerged by the incursion of rivers or of the sea, so the mind of a Christian, divinely illuminated by faith—wherein is to be found the knowledge of the wise, and without which there is no true wisdom—is sometimes so surrounded with floods of light, that it is necessarily lost therein, by reason both of their abundance and their brightness. This truth is marvellously displayed in the revelation which Christianity makes to us of the holy angels; and we may truly say that this science of love and of those admirable spirits is a holy and divine inundation. We have but to think of it seriously for a moment, and a host of reasons will crowd in upon the mind, overwhelming it with their force and multitude; it is, indeed, an abyss of love in which we lose ourselves. We discover so many motives and so many reasons to love these spirits, who are all love, and all these motives are so touching, and all these reasons so urgent, that we feel altogether bewildered. We desire to declare them because the zeal of our devotion impels us to do so, and we are unable to express them. It is the property of great things to be unutterable. This illumination causes a species of martyrdom in the soul which loves; it is wonderful how its love increases its light, and how the light it receives increases its love ; and how, by virtue of its very greatness, this love at last makes the soul feel as though it were powerless to love, because, love prompting it to make known the dear object of its affections, the great knowledge it possesses thereof takes away from it the power of expressing how lovely it is. It rejoices, however, in the thought that the holy motives which dispose our hearts to love the good angels are greater than language can convey ; and this thought brings with it a sweet satisfaction; for it is much to say of these sublime intelligences, that it is not possible worthily to declare their excellencies. But after all, love is a fire which cannot be hid, sooner or later it must burst forth ; and if it is difficult to know how to speak of devotion to the holy angels, it would be still more difficult to be silent.

In a word, then, all possible motives, all imaginable reasons, urge us to love these spirits of love, and to such a degree, that a man must surely have neither mind to reflect nor heart to love, or he must confess that nothing can be more just than devotion to the holy angels, and that they ought to be loved at any rate. Thus I have always said, As for me, I am not afraid of not loving the holy angels—always supposing the aid of divine grace—for that seems to me impossible; but I am afraid of not loving them enough. God, on His part, obligee us thereto, and the creature also obliges us : this is, to say everything in few words. If you regard God, you must love the angels; if you regard the creature, if you regard yourself, you must love them. Pure love commands it; self-love requires it ; God Only wills it; the most holy Virgin and all the Saints desire it ; our own pleasure and satisfaction, our own interest, demand it.

If you have given yourself to God only, you must give yourself to the holy angels ; if your love is mixed with self-interest, that again obliges you to be devout to them. In truth, the hearts of men are moved to love in very different ways. There are some, but they are few in number, who possess a generosity of spirit so divine, that, looking no longer in a manner at what concerns themselves, neither at temporal nor spiritual interests, neither at heaven nor hell, time nor eternity, regarding neither their own salvation nor their own glory, in an entire forgetfulness of self, they look to God alone. God alone is their only all in all things. God alone it is who is their motive in everything ; it is He alone whom they desire in life, in death, and after death. There are others, again, who look to God and love Him ; but at the same time that they have an eye to God and to His love, they have an eye to their own interests. The hearts of some are attracted by beauty, others are led by honour, others again are allured by profit. You will see some impressed by greatness, or captivated by extraordinary excellencies and perfections ; others again who are won upon by constant love, faithful services, and particular obligations. Thus men who have hearts, and hearts which love, are attracted to love in very different ways ; as they have not the same inclinations, so neither are they moved to love by the same considerations. Ho who loves profit will not trouble himself so much about honour, because the things that are most honourable are often not the most useful ; and so again, he who loves honour will despise money ; he will not set his heart upon it like the miser ; he must spend in order to attain that eminence to which glory leads him to aspire. But were there anything in the world which could equally bestow riches, honour, and pleasure, assuredly it would be loved greatly by all.

Here, then, O men ! I call you to love and devotion for the holy angels. Every kind of good is to be found in their love. If you love God, you must love the angels; if you love the rare perfections with which God has endowed creatures, you must love the angels ; if you love yourselves, you must love them ; if temporal things interest you, their services in this respect are beyond belief. If you love pleasure, honour, and profit, these blessed spirits will procure them for you in this life, provided it be for the glory of their Master or the good of your soul; but it is perfectly certain that they will obtain for you in eternity pleasures which surpass all human thought, as well as honours and treasures inestimable. If you desire the patronage of the powerful, there is nothing more powerful among created beings than the angelic nature. If you desire the consideration of the great, ah ! they are the great princes of the empyrean, the princes and the kings of a glorious eternity. But that which is very sweet to think upon is that they share their crowns with their friends ; they make them their associates in power : to be a true friend of the angels is to be on the certain road to a kingdom, and to be well assured of receiving one day the sceptre and the diadem of an imperishable glory. Ah ! how unlike is their conduct to that of the great of this world, who set their hearts upon nothing so much as upon reigning alone ; while what these princes of love most ardently desire is to have companions in their empire. If your heart is captivated by beauty, they are pre-eminently beautiful ; but their beauty is not like to that earthly beauty which is but on the surface of the skin, and which an illness effaces : their loveliness is unchangeable, and remains for ever unchanged. But as the matter of salvation is of the last importance, it is in this one great business that we receive from them the most extraordinary assistance.

In fine, they are friends matchless in merit, in love, in constancy. Their merits, their perfections, and their excellence no pen can describe, no mouth, however eloquent, can declare. Their love for men is altogether marvellous, for it comprises every kind of love. Their constancy is incredible, since they are never weary of loving us, whatever cause of displeasure we may give them. They keep untiring watch over everything which concerns us. They serve us as a fortress against the power of the devils. They are our protection and our defence against all our other enemies. They are all at the service of all men, and that for every manner of service, however vile and abject it may be. Great truths these in few words !

In short, if you belong to the number of those pure souls who act only according as the Spirit of Jesus Christ moves them, and who regard God only, you must, as we have already said, love the angels; and whither could our inclinations lead us with more justice and holiness than towards these objects of the sweetest complacency of God? If it be true that the love of God must be the rule of our love, how exalted should be our love for the angels, who are the matchless creations of the love of God ! Assuredly we often deceive ourselves in the objects of our friendship, but in loving what God loves, and as God wills we should love, we cannot possibly be deceived. Whichever way, then, we turn, we find ourselves constrained to have devotion to the holy angels. The heart of man must change its nature, or he cannot but love the angels ; for whither shall he go to escape angelic love? If he ascend up to heaven, there he will meet with those enrapturing splendours of a blessed eternity ; and their beauty is irresistible : it must conquer him, or he must cease to love. If he make the circuit of the earth, and seek the farthest limits of the world, all elements, fire, air, water, earth, and all that he finds therein, proclaim aloud the love of these sovereigns of love. The sun in his perpetual course, which a presiding angel guides, announces every day this love from one end of the world to the other, and that bright orb, with its illuminating rays, plainly declares this truth to all creatures here below. The dawn which precedes the rising of the sun publishes from the very break of day the loving care of these spiritual lights, the morning stars of creation; and the night is never dark enough to hide their goodness. The light of these divine stars knows no setting. Stationed on the walls of the mystic Jerusalem, these sentinels watch by night as well as by day. If we go down to the very centre of the earth, we shall see, amidst the fires of Purgatory, the love of these charitable spirits burning with more intensity even than the purifying flames. Countries the most forsaken receive assistance from them. These suns of the empyrean rise upon sinners as well as on the just. There lives not a pagan, not a savage, not one reasonable creature, however mean and wretched, but has an angel for his guardian. They are to be found in the vilest hovels of the most degraded beings on earth, as well as in the palaces of princes; every soul experiences their help; all nature is assisted by them; in short, it may be truly said that on every side we behold the triumph of their love.

How is it possible, then, to resist so many charms, so many sweet and powerful motives? O ye sons of men! how long will you be dull of heart? How long will you love everything but what you ought to love? We can but weep over the insensibility and blindness of men. These are undoubted truths, and it is evident that we have every conceivable motive to love the holy angels. Nevertheless, devotion to them is very rare ; and if these spirits are very loving, they are also very little loved. It is true that devotion to our angel guardians, who generally belong to the lowest choir, begins to be more common; but there are few who practise devotion to all the other choirs of these celestial hierarchies. Few cultivate any love to the Seraphim, the Cherubim, the Thrones, the Dominations, the Virtues, the Powers, the Principalities, and the Archangels.

I know that this defect is to be ascribed to the absence of the interior life in the majority of souls. They are all immersed in the flesh, and nothing but the things of sense affect them ; there are few who, by their detachment from material objects, and their perfect disengagement of spirit, give scope to those pure elevations of grace which raise our minds to a heavenly conversation, while our bodies still live here below upon earth, and which, by revealing to us the spiritual world, fix our attention on what passes there. Looking upon our guardian angels as near to us—and this is so far well ; indeed, we cannot think too much about them—and regarding them as ever watchful to procure for us that which is good, and to deliver us from evil, we feel a little more interest about them ; and yet, after all, the return we make is as nothing when we attentively consider the extraordinary obligations we owe them. But why not cultivate a friendship with the Seraphim, the Cherubim, and all the other angels? The more exalted they are, the greater is their power as well as their love ; and, what ought to move us still more, there is more of God in them, which is the one great motive with those souls who love God purely. You, who read these pages, tell me if the kings of the earth were willing to receive you to their private friendship, and to place you in the number of their greatest favourites, what would you do? Examine your heart a little upon this question, and let it be honestly; then reflect that it rests solely with yourself to contract sweet and everlasting friendships with a countless number of the kings of heaven; it rests solely with yourself to enjoy their highest favour. If you do but desire it—and I conjure you to reflect repeatedly on this truth—it will be your own fault if, through their interest, you do not become, like them, kings in the blessed abode of the empyrean.

Truly it would be my desire to use every possible means, with the help of divine grace, to arouse the minds of men, and bring them in some measure out of their state of blindness on the subject of devotion to all the choirs of angels. It is this motive which has prompted me to compose this little book in their honour. I have long been pressed to do so, not only by excellent persons to whom I owe deference, but much more by those inward solicitations which I have experienced. For more than fourteen or fifteen years I have felt myself so strongly urged thereto, and with so many proofs that it is the All-Good God who asks me to undertake this little task, that I should consider myself to be very unfaithful to grace were I to resist. After composing my other little works of "God Only," "The Love of Jesus in the Most Holy Sacrament," and "Devotion to the Most Admirable Mother of God," it is but just that I should write of love and devotion to the nine choirs of holy angels. I shall be reminded, perhaps, that the number of devotional books is already large, but a great Saint of our days, the glorious Francis de Sales, has long ago replied to this objection. Alas! we never hear it made matter of complaint that people are almost always speaking of earth; for do but take notice, and you will observe that almost the whole conversation in society turns upon the objects of sense. The earth, and the men who inhabit it, the pleasures and the profits of this world, form well-nigh the whole occupation of minds and hearts, and consequently the whole subject-matter of their conversation and writings.

Just reflect a moment seriously how few there are in any single city whose conversation is of God, and of those precious ways which lead to the blessed fruition of Him, as poverty, chastity, mortification, or self-denial. How many letters are written every day in all parts of the world ! And is it not true that almost all these letters have reference only to the affairs of earth?—letters about lawsuits, rents, farms, money, letters to promote the writer's establishment in the world, to keep up his interest with creatures, to secure their friendship and esteem, and to avoid their contempt and estrangement—in short, for the honour and glory of this miserable world : yet who complains of all these letters? But O the blindness and frightful insensibility of creatures, O darkness and hardness of heart, worthy of tears of blood : people cry out that too many writings are devoted to the love, the honour, and the interest of God ! How abominable in all things are thy ways, O world ! I resolve never to entertain for thee anything but horror, and every imaginable aversion. I do not trouble myself, therefore, about what thou thinkest, or mayest think or say: God only, God only, God only—and He suffices me. Thy esteem, O world, and thy friendship, and all thy talk, do not deserve a moment's thought, unless it be to detest them. If we are told that all the little things we say in these books of ours are very worthless, we most readily agree ; we believe and say the same thing : but this it is that makes us look for greater blessings from heaven; the less there is to expect from the creature, the more there is to be looked for from God. My very nothingness supports me, for I know that God has drawn His greatest works out of nothing.

Trusting, then, solely in Jesus, in the protection of His most holy Mother, and in the powerful and charitable assistance of the holy angels, I dedicate this little work to the glory of those blessed spirits. Willingly would I have gone from city to city, and from village to village, publishing the goodness of the angels, and the motives which oblige us to love them. Gladly would I have spoken of them in the ears of all men had it been in my power, and cried aloud everywhere, both in public resorts and in all other places, "Come ye all, and join in love and devotion to the angels." But at least, since this is not possible, I publish these pages, that they may supply for my silence, and reach where I cannot make myself heard; so that, being myself incapable of any great thing, or, to speak more correctly, being unable to do anything at all, I may at least do what I can, in the power of God's grace, to inspire the hearts of men with love for the angelic choirs.

In old time the divine Chrysostom, reflecting on the misery of the world, expressed a wish that those words of Ecclesiastes (i. 2), "Vanity of vanities, and all is vanity," which so emphatically mark its nothingness, were written up in large characters in public places, on the gates of cities, on the doors of houses, everywhere. And for my part, I would wish that the words of that great Pope, St Leo, "*Confirmate amicitias cum sanctis angelis,*" "Make friendships with the holy angels," should be written up in the streets of towns and villages, in all our churches, in all apartments and private chambers; that everywhere there should be persons whose business it was to repeat them again and again ; that no preachers should ever deliver a sermon without proclaiming them aloud ; and that they should be constantly introduced into private conversation.

Do what we will, we shall never worthily acquit ourselves of our duties towards these amiable spirits. Hence it is that the holy Fathers omit nothing which may lead us to honour and love them. Sometimes they press us to cultivate their holy love, and form sweet friendships with them, familiarising ourselves with their company ; sometimes they exhort us to pay our homage to them, and to honour them to the best of our ability. Sometimes they remind us not to forget their presence, to be careful to respect them, to think of them, and hold converse with them; and in other places, they charge us to be exceedingly thankful to them for their kindness, and never let the memory of it be effaced from our minds : in short, they use all their endeavours to excite us to practise so fitting a devotion.

The heavenly St Denis, who has written so lovingly of them, delights in assuming the title of Philangelus, that is to say, the Friend of the Angels. This man of God, contemporary of the Apostles, and disciple of the great St Paul, full of the apostolic spirit, and of the love of the angels, who are the Apostles of Heaven, and coadjutors of apostolic men on earth, in order to demonstrate to us and to all posterity his zeal for these admirable spirits, publicly takes the appellation of their friend, and inscribes it in his writings, that all the world may know it.

Let each man desire what he will; for my part, if there be in the world an enviable title, to my taste it is that of Philangelus, the Friend of Angels. O title far surpassing that of monarch or sovereign ! O quality more precious than gold, than topazes, and all the most splendid jewels this world affords ! Is there anything one ought not willingly to do and to suffer to acquire so glorious an attribute? O spirits worthy of all love ! my highest ambition shall ever be to attain the exalted honour of your holy friendship. I love you, and desire to love you; but make me to love you more. I have nothing to offer more valuable than my heart : I give it you, then, and place it in your hands, that you may direct it, and mould it to pure love ; that it may love in unison with you, and may love only what you love, and as you love—God only. I have nothing more precious than my life : I dedicate it to your glory; and I should reckon myself too happy were I to lose it for your honour in honour of God ; at least, I have dedicated every moment of it to God for your glory. I desire to praise you unceasingly, in life, in death, and after death. I possess nothing larger than my desires. Ah ! they are all yours, and I could wish that the whole earth might echo to your praises; that everywhere there were temples, and in all these temples altars consecrated to you; everywhere congregations, processions established, sermons, preachers employed, pens devoted to your service ; that everywhere your pictures were displayed; everywhere festivals celebrated, offices composed in your honour ; holy fraternities of persons whose profession it was to make you known, to remind men of your sweet presence, and lead them to salute you, and whose great business it should be speak of you, and to call upon all the world to love you, and to love God only in you, who is the Great All, who alone is to be honoured in all things.

But since such things surpass my power, I will at least do all I can ; at least I will declare in these pages that you are all-amiable, all-loving, and, alas ! very little loved. I will cry aloud to all who read them, "Come ye and join in love and devotion to the angels." O ye men, love the angels ; they are friends pre-eminently faithful, powerful advocates and protectors, most wise masters, fathers, brothers, all filled with love for us. They are the patrons, protectors, and advocates of all men without distinction, of every state and of every class. Love the angels, ye apostolic men; they are the heavenly missionaries of Paradise. Love the angels, ye preachers and doctors, for they are the adepts in heavenly science, and in the ravishing eloquence of eternity. Love the angels, ye who are the priests of the Lord; it is by their hands that the Sacrifice is offered to the Divine Majesty. Love the angels, ye who dwell in the retirement of cloisters, or in the seclusion of solitude; these admirable spirits are always retired in God, and always behold His face. Love the angels, ye who appear in public, who live amidst the world; these pure intelligences abide there with you. Love the angels, ye married persons; the example of the holy Archangel Raphael, who conducted Tobias, admirably displays the care they take of your state. Love the angels, ye widows and orphans; for none may be compared to them in the charitable help they give to those who need. Love the angels, O virgins—yes, I repeat it, love the angels with fervour, O ye virgins; they are the great friends of virginity; nay, they are its admirers, beholding this precious treasure in fragile vessels, and creatures so weak living on earth as they themselves live in heaven. Love the angels, O ye just; they are the guides of holiness. Love the angels, O ye sinners; they are for you a sure refuge. Love the angels, ye who are afflicted, who are poor and in misery; they are the consolation and resource of all who sorrow. Love the angels, ye rich and powerful, ye great ones of this world; these are the heavenly luminaries who will enlighten you to see that all which passes is contemptible, and that you should sigh only after a blessed eternity. Yes, O men! love the Seraphim; they are the princes of pure love. Love the Cherubim; they are the great doctors of the science of the saints. Love the Thrones; they are the patrons of true repose of soul and tranquil peace of heart. Love the Dominations; they will teach you to become masters of yourselves and of all things, raising you above all created beings by an intimate union with the Creator. Love the Virtues; they are the masters of the ways of holy perfection. Love the Powers; they are your defenders against the malice, the rage, and the power of the devils. Love the Principalities; it is they who watch so diligently over the welfare of kingdoms, states, and those who govern.

Love the Archangels ; for they are zealous for the common good, and we receive at their hands benefits without number in provinces, towns, and villages, and in every part of the world. Love, in fine, the Angels of the last choir; they are stars whose celestial influences we feel the more often because they are nearer to us, watching over the good of each one of us in particular with an ineffable love and care. Henceforth let our love be as of fire for these pure flames of love empyreal, and let us never cease from loving those who are never weary of doing us good, and loading us with every favour.

Bless, O my God ! all who are devout to Thy holy angels, and all who, on reading these pages, shall earnestly resolve to practise this devotion. Bless them with the blessing of the just, directing them along those straight paths which lead to Thee, and withdrawing them from the crooked paths of sinners. Bless them with the blessing of Abraham, giving them the spirit of sacrifice, of self-immolation, and oblation. Bless them with the blessing of Isaac, teaching them obedience and submission to Thy divine will. Bless them with the blessing of Jacob, manifesting to them the mysteries of holy religion. Bless them with the blessing of the elect, so that they may hear those sweet words, "Come, ye blessed of My Father, possess the kingdom prepared for you from the foundation of the world." Bless them with the blessing of these heavenly spirits, joining them to their society, and giving them to partake of their happiness. Great and august Queen of Paradise ! bless them with thy loving protection, so that, all being united in one and the same great object, the glory of God only, God only may live and reign in all our hearts to everlasting ages.

Note

[1] "Scientia sapientis tanquam inundatio abundabit," xxi. 16.

PART I.

MOTIVES FOR THIS DEVOTION.

FIRST MOTIVE.

The Admirable Perfections of these Sublime Intelligences.

The excellences of the angels are like a fathomless and, as it were, shoreless ocean. It is, as I have said, an abyss in which the mind necessarily loses itself. Souls duly enlightened know well that what they say is far below what they think of them, and that what they think is far below the reality; for true indeed it is that their greatness is as far beyond the thought of man to conceive as it is beyond his words to express. The angelic nature is a whole world of perfections in itself ; and when to this is superadded the state of grace and glory, it is beyond measure admirable. It is a certain truth that the nature of men, however great its perfection, is inferior to that of angels, for this we learn from Holy Scripture; but a theologian of weight[1] has taught, what, however, is not the received opinion, that the lowest of the angels in the state of glory is above the highest of the saints ; and it is in this sense that he explains those words of Holy Writ (Matt. xi. 11), which say that he who is the lesser in the kingdom of heaven is greater than John the Baptist. But besides the incomparable Mother of God, who without doubt is exalted above all the choirs of angels, he excepted the glorious St Joseph, on account of his belonging to an 1 St Ambrose. order differing from that of all other saints, because of the extraordinary office which he filled in connexion with the hypostatic union, being honoured with the title of husband of the Mother of God, reputed father of the God-Man, and, in a manner, saviour of the Saviour.

This, at least, we know, that the angels are spiritual substances, incorruptible by nature, perfectly separate from matter, and entirely free from all those infirmities which compass us on every side. They are spirits all brightness; they are acquainted with all the secrets of nature; and all that has remained most hidden from the greatest minds that have ever existed is intimately known to them. They know things without labour, and countless things at the same time, and in an instant of time, unaccompanied with doubt or obscurity. They do not make use of discourse like men, nor comprehend the things they know after our manner—that is, by reasoning from one thing to another ; they understand everything at a glance, and this is why they are styled emphatically *Intelligences.* Scripture describes them as habited in a garment of brightness and of fire,[1] to indicate to us the spiritual light with which they are endowed; it clothes them, in the Apocalypse (i. 13-16), with a robe like to that of the high priests of old, to show us that the most sacred mysteries of religion are revealed to them. In fine, it represents them as enveloped with clouds,[2] to teach us that their brilliancy is too intense for our minds to endure—we can behold it only under a veil—the eye of man has not strength to gaze upon it. The wisest men upon earth are but children in comparison with these pure intelligences.

Their power also is inconceivable. One single angel could defeat millions of men set in battle array, yea, all the men in the world united together; he could work marvellous changes in the elements, in cities, provinces, and kingdoms. The angels can make the winds to blow, rain to fall, thunder to roar; they can raise tempests, cause earthquakes, stop the course of rivers, bestow abundance, or produce a famine, cure all maladies, or inflict incurable disorders, fashion themselves bodies, and perform a thousand other wonders, the causes of which men know not ; and all this they can effect almost in a moment of time. They are represented with wings,[1] to denote their swiftness, which exceeds that of the heavens and of the winds ; in an instant they pass from one end of the world to another, thus making themselves ubiquitous, as Tertullian says.

But their loveliness is perfectly enchanting; that which is fairest upon earth being mere deformity compared with their celestial beauty. The angels are all beauty ; the least beautiful among them surpassing in loveliness all the united charms of earth. The mind is utterly lost in the thought of the infinite assemblage of beauty composing these angelic choirs ; for if the angels differ from one another in kind, and consequently each has his own peculiar beauty, and if the lowest possesses more than all earthly creatures, and if, on the other hand, their number is, in a manner, infinite, a multitude which no man can number, and which is known only to God—O my God, what countless beauties does the Heavenly Sion contain ! But O how dazzling must be the splendour of the most exalted spirits of this glorious city ! And here St Anselm's words are often quoted, who, to give us some idea of these truths by means of sensible objects, says, that were God to put an angel in the place of the sun, and surround him with as many suns as there are stars, and were He to permit this blessed spirit to transfuse into the form he has assumed some rays of his own brightness, he would eclipse all the splendour of these suns, and render them invisible to our eyes. A learned man has opined that the sun itself, which enlightens this world, has no other light but that which it receives from the angel who moves and guides it; for, says he, though the angel does not inform this luminary, and acts towards it only as an assistant form, it is very possible that he imparts to it all its brilliancy, even as the blood in the human frame, in the opinion of those who do not believe it to be animated, nevertheless receives from the soul a certain lustre, which it loses when the soul is separated from the body.

In a word, everything about these amiable spirits is enrapturing. An angel appeared to St Francis, and for his entertainment played upon a musical instrument He touched it but once, yet so melodiously, that the saint afterwards declared, that had he continued he must have died of such an excess of sweetness. That miraculous bird, whose song once so enchanted a religious who served God in the retirement of a desert, that he passed several centuries in that solitude without weariness, and with so much pleasure that he imagined he had spent only a quarter of an hour, God preserving him miraculously all this time, was no doubt an angel who took the form of a bird. Father Cornelius à Lapide asserts that, being desirous to examine into the truth of this miracle, he made a journey on purpose to the spot where it was said to have occurred, and to the monastery to which the afore-named religious belonged, and that, after having made a most careful examination into the matter, he had found very satisfactory evidence of its truth.*

This is also one reason why the angels were created in the empyreal heaven ; it was most fitting that such noble and perfect creatures should take their origin in a heaven which is the abode of all enjoyment and blessedness. All those precious stones which were shown of old to the Prophet Ezekiel (i. 26, 27), typified to us the various perfections of the angels. The holy Fathers outdo themselves when it is question of bestowing titles and praises on them. To express all in one word, they may be called pure and lustrous mirrors reflecting God : they are at once His brilliant mirrors and His most lively images ; their excellence is indeed without shade of imperfection. Alas ! it is not thus with the little perfection which is to be seen here below on earth, and which is to be found only with a wretched alloy of faults and weaknesses. The nobility of the angels is unsullied by meanness, their knowledge is without ignorance, their light without darkness, their power without weakness, their beauty without the least blemish, their love without taint, their will without inconstancy, their peace without disturbance, their activity without intermission, their operation incessant and without toil, their designs without anxiety, their happiness without fear, their blessedness consummate in every respect without the least admixture of evil.

It is related in the Book of Judges (xiii. 18), that Manue having asked an angel who appeared to him what was his name, he replied that his name was "Wonderful." In the 16th chapter of Genesis, Agar, as Scripture tells us (ver. 13), called the name of the Lord who spake to her, "Thou the God who hast seen me." Now it was an angel who at that time spake to her, but this title is ascribed to angels, because they represent God so admirably. Hence in the same book of Genesis, chapter 31st, Jacob says (ver. 30) that he has seen God face to face, when speaking of the angel who had appeared to him. With all these perfections, can men refuse the angels the love which is due to them—men who are so disposed to love what is beautiful and noble and perfect? This truth well deserves to be pondered long and deeply, to the glory of God, the Author of all these excellences and all these perfections.

Notes

[1] *E.g.,* Ezek. i. 13, 14 ; Matt. xxviii. 3.

[2] *E.g.,* Ezek. i. 4.

[1] E.g., Isa. vi. 2 ; Ezek. i. 8, &c.

* See Note A.

SECOND MOTIVE.

The Incomparable Goodness of these Spirits or Love.

"Nothing so touches a good heart as to see itself beloved," says the holy Bishop of Geneva, in his book on "The Love of God;" but the motives for a return of love are much increased when the person who loves us is one of exalted character. If this be so, we must either love the angels or give up loving. We have but just now seen that their power, their knowledge, their beauty, are beyond compare; add to this, that they are great princes, yea, kings, who reign with the Sovereign King of Eternity over an empire which knows no end. Consider, moreover, that these amiable princes of the blessed Paradise not only love us, but love us with every different kind of love, and this to such a degree, that it would appear as if they had resolved that none should surpass them in love.

It may be truly said that they are the passionate lovers of men. They love us, then, these lords of the empyrean, with a father's love: being always anxious for our advancement, and the promotion of our welfare; always filled with the desire of procuring us some benefit; never ceasing to do us good ; looking upon our interests as their own; labouring with inexpressible care to obtain for us a large share in the high honours of a glorious eternity; and neglecting nothing to secure to us the inheritance of glory which has been purchased for us by the mercies of the Adorable Jesus. They love us with a mother's love : for it is written (Ps. xc. 12) that they shall "bear" us "in their hands." Like a good mother, who folds her child to her bosom, they carry us in their arms ; they watch over both our bodies and our souls ; they keep their eyes always fixed upon us, and caress us with all the tenderness which a holy love inspires. They love us with a brother's love : for they look upon us as their younger brethren ; and, what is indeed most wonderful and rare, worthier of heaven than of earth, not only do our holy guardians feel no displeasure at seeing us their equals in glory, but they are delighted that it should be so, and do all they can that they may behold us more glorious in Paradise than they are themselves. They love us with the love of a passionate lover : always thinking of us, always striving to win our love ; never losing sight of us day or night ; abandoning even the delightful abode of heaven in order to abide with us continually on earth; and desiring and seeking our good more than their own. They love us with the love of a vigilant pastor : for is it not of these blessed spirits that it may be said that "they who keep Israel neither slumber nor sleep" ?[1] They love us with the love of a kind physician : for they dress our wounds, heal our maladies, restore us to health, and all with an incomparable gentleness. They love us with the love of a pleader and an advocate : devoting themselves with goodness unspeakable to all our affairs, both heavenly and earthly, but especially to the great affair of eternity. They love us with the love of a faithful guide : conducting us with marvellous love through all the painful ways of this life, and preserving us from the precipices which surround us on all sides. They love us with the love of a good master : keeping us under their protection, and enabling us to earn rewards exceeding beyond all proportion the small services we render them. They love us with the love of a wise and patient doctor : teaching us the science of the saints and the high doctrine of Jesus Christ. They love us with the love of a good king : defending us from our enemies, causing us to live in peace, and keeping us in all security. In a word, they love us as much as it is possible for them to love us.

Behold, then, how our hearts are constrained to love, seeing themselves beloved in such various ways by creatures so noble, so beautiful, so powerful, so perfect,—these mighty kings of Paradise ! But when did they begin to love us ? From the very moment that we came into being. And how long has their friendship lasted? Without intermission, during every single instant of our life. Will it be enduring? It will endure to our last breath, and, if we will, even after death, for ever, for ever, as long as God is God, throughout a long and never-ending eternity. Do they love us in all things? In all things whatsoever which concern our true happiness. And is there no exception ? None whatever. And what do they do to advance our good? They do all they can; no employment seems too vile or abject for them when it is question of serving us. In what places do they labour for our good? In every place, country, and land, wherever we go, in heaven itself, and under the earth, in the midst of the fires and flames of Purgatory. Does not our ingratitude repel them ? No; they remain unchangeably attached to our service, without disgust, without weariness, whatever cause we may give them to the contrary.

It is true, then, that the holy angels are our oldest friends, that their love is the most constant, the most faithful, the most sweet, the most patient, the most universal that can be. All therein is great, all is enchanting, all is admirable, and, let us add, all is disinterested : for what do they receive from men ? Ingratitude beyond conception, insolent contempt, shameful neglect. The heathen know them not; heretics know them without paying them the respect which is their due; the greater part of the poor country-people know as little of them as the heathen. Often they who know most about them neglect them most; they who pass for loving them think of them at times, and on occasions honour them; and here we see the whole extent of the love of men for these spirits, who are ever near them, and ever thinking of them. These truths, seriously meditated upon from time to time, will fill the soul with profound amazement, as it compares the exceeding love displayed by the angels towards men with the exceeding ingratitude and coldness evinced by men towards the angels. Once again, then, let us ask, Whence is it, O heavenly spirits, that ye love these men, and wherefore do ye desire their love? Here every mind must stand confounded. Let him who can fathom this mystery; for my part, I confess that the love of the angels is past all understanding. Fain would I go through the earth exclaiming against the ingratitude and the insensibility of the human heart. Truly it must be confessed that herein the ingratitude of man is displayed in all its blackness, and the hardness of his heart in its most revolting form. O men, rouse yourselves from this unhappy state, and surrender yourselves at length to all these attractions of love. Love the angels, love the God of the angels; for it is in Him alone that all is to be loved that is worthy of love.

Note

[1] Ps. cxx. 4.

THIRD MOTIVE.

All the Holy Angels are Engaged in the Service of Men.

I confess that as I proceed to write of the love of the angels, my heart feels itself becoming gradually more and more softened: and if they are fires and flames of fire, as Scripture teaches us (Ps. ciii. 4; comp. Heb. i. 7), I marvel not that my heart should be all dissolved, to express myself in the Psalmist's words (xxi. 15), like wax that melts at the fire. O amiable spirits ! suffer my poor soul to pour itself forth in love : either let me die, or let me love you to my heart's content. Let me with you love with pure love Jesus, the King, and Mary, the Queen of holy love. Either I must cease to love, or I must live only by this pure love.

But how fitted are the motives, which here we can but merely glance at, to dispose us to this love ! We have said that the angels love men with every variety of love, and that they love them with an inviolable fidelity and a matchless patience; but how many of these amiable princes are engaged in their service? Some few, perhaps, from among their heavenly bands ? Let us listen to the divine Paul in answer to our question, who says (Heb. i. 14) that *all* are ministering spirits, sent for our salvation. St Augustine teaches that all the angels watch over us, because we constitute with them one only City of God, of which one portion, composed of men, yet wayfarers on earth, is assisted by the other portion, the angels, who live in the blessed fruition of their true end. When we say that the angels watch over the salvation of men, says the eloquent St John Chrysostom, we must not be supposed to speak only of the angels of the lowest choirs, but even of the most exalted and the highest.

It may, indeed, be asked whether the angels of the first choirs descend here below to assist men. Some doctors are of opinion that they do not, but it is difficult for them to explain away the testimony of Scripture to the contrary. St Raphael, who acted as guide to the young Tobias, testified (Tob. xii. 15) that he was "one of the seven princes who stand before the Lord." Cherubim appeared to the Prophet Ezekiel (chap.

x.); a seraph purified the lips of Isaiah (vi. 2-7); we read also in Genesis (iii. 24), that God has committed to a cherub the guardianship of the earthly Paradise; thus it is evident that the angels even of the first choirs are sent here below for the guidance of men. The lives of the Saints teach us this same truth. It was a seraph who imprinted the wounds of our merciful Saviour on the body of St Francis; it was a seraph also who wounded with a dart of love the heart of the seraphic Teresa. But this is not the essential point ; it suffices that it is an undoubted truth that all, without exception, take care of us in one way or another. All the nine choirs of angels are engaged in the service of men.

Now the number of the angels is so exceedingly great that the holy man Job (xxv. 3) declares them to be innumerable. There are learned men who maintain that they surpass in number all the stars of heaven, all the birds of the air, all the drops of water, all the blades of grass, all the atoms, in fine, which compose this visible creation. St Gregory of Nyssa says that there are infinite millions of them; that is to say, to the mind of man, their multitude is as if infinite, and is known to God alone. He alone, says the great St Denis, knows their number.

What strong and lively emotions of love do our poor hearts experience, and how are they filled with consolation, when they have well penetrated these truths ! Reader, were you to be told that the king had despatched one of the first princes of his court on purpose to attend upon you, and to render you every possible service, what feelings would be yours, what sentiments of gratitude ! Could you contain your joy? and what would be your amazement, what the surprise, the delight, of all your relatives and friends ! But history records nothing of the kind; earth can display nothing so gracious; such favours are reserved for Heaven : it belongs only to the God of Paradise to perform these prodigies of love. O my soul! O my soul ! have we ever seriously thought of this? Hast thou ever well considered that all the princes of the court of the King of kings interest themselves in thy affairs, are set to guard thee, and watch with goodness ineffable over everything which concerns thee? It is true that one among these princes is thy more immediate guardian, nevertheless Scripture informs us that "all are ministering spirits, sent for them who shall receive the inheritance of salvation." O the love of God who has sent them! O the love of these princes who are sent! What consolation to our poor souls! Why after this should they be sad? Why should they be ever troubled? The presence of a single one of these princes ought to be sufficient to remove from us all fear, and raise our courage, however much we may be cast down; and behold millions, thousands of millions, countless millions—to use the words of the Fathers, numbers without number! O my heart! consider that if one such powerful protector is sufficient to insure thy safety, the friendship of all these illustrious lords of the empyrean may well serve to fill and occupy thee. Ah, what time, or what room shall we have remaining for earth? Assuredly there are too many sweet friendships to contract in Heaven with the angels for us to amuse ourselves here below with men; and how pure and holy are these friendships, seeing that they are formed with pure spirits, in whom we find God only!

FOURTH MOTIVE.
All Men are Assisted by the Holy Angels.

We need seek no other reason for the love of God but that love itself, as our Lord revealed to the Venerable Mother Magdalen of St Joseph, a Carmelite nun of eminent sanctity; for why does God thus love men? Let it be published among the nations, says the devout St Bernard, and let them confess that the Lord has resolved to deal magnificently with them. O Lord! what is man, that Thou shouldst deign to make Thyself known to him, and to bestow upon him the love of Thy heart? Thou lovest him; Thou takest care of him; Thou givest to him Thine Only Son; Thou sendest to him Thy Holy Spirit; and that there may remain nothing in Heaven which is not occupied with his welfare, Thou deputest the blessed spirits to watch over him, to minister to him, and to instruct him. Behold, then, the angel, who is a great king, full of perfections, beauty, and glory, devoted to the service of man, who is one mass of imperfections, foulness, and wretchedness ; of man who is nothing but a vile insect, a worm of the earth, a heap of corruption, the food of worms, a little clay and mud, a leaf which the wind carries away. And, what is still more surprising, the angel is engaged in the service of man, a sinner !

The Divine Word teaches us (1 John i. 8), "that if we say that we have not sinned, we deceive ourselves, and the truth is not in us." The holiest fall into deplorable venial sins, though it be not with full advertence ; and venial sin is an offence against God : this is why souls who have truly given themselves to God fall into them only by surprise ; they would rather suffer all imaginable torments in this life, and even in the next, than commit one such sin with their eyes open, that is, with full knowledge and deliberate purpose. Hell, said the devout St Anselm, would be to me more endurable than the very smallest sin. They who love God will well understand this truth; the rest will scarcely comprehend it. But more than this : not only venial sin, but the least shadow of venial sin, according to the opinion of the loving and divine Catherine of Genoa, would be capable of crushing to atoms that man who should thoroughly understand its true nature, had he even a body as hard as diamond, and this at the slightest glimpse which might be given him of it. So true it is, that the smallest offence against God has in it something fearful ; no language can express how horrible a thing is sin. Oh, if men did but know what they do when they relapse into it ! Now the angels, these spirits who are all light, discern the abominableness of it far more clearly than do the most enlightened souls, and yet they cease not to assist, with incredible kindness, those who are infected with this dreadful disease.

Soul ! whoever you may be who read these truths, pause a while, I entreat you, to reflect upon them. It is a wonderful thing, this goodness of the angels, who refuse not to bestow their care upon those who allow themselves to commit offences, however slight, against their Creator; considering the knowledge they possess of the most adorable greatness of the Divine Majesty, which is insulted thereby. How amazing, then, to see that they abandon not those wretches who live in mortal sin,—Deicides, who trample under foot the Blood of a God, and are guilty of His Death : those traitors against the Majesty of God, those children, those members, those slaves of the devil, those captives of hell!

But this is not all. Heretics and unbelievers have angels to guard them. That great saint, Teresa, said that the soul of a Catholic in mortal sin was like a fair mirror, whose purity is wholly sullied and entirely spoilt, so that it is now a hideous object; but that this mirror in heretics is not only spoilt but broken. The supernatural lights with which this seraphic soul was favoured taught her deep truths under the form of similitudes, of which she made use for the instruction of others. The plague of heresy is a raging evil, which we shall never fully comprehend till we arrive at that eternal country where truth shall be beheld in all its solidity and splendour. But, after all, the love of the angels bears even with this; they watch over these miserable beings, over all unbelievers, pagans, and idolaters. Turks, who are their avowed enemies, since they are the enemies of the very name of Christian, receive their aid. Even Antichrist shall have a guardian angel, according to the doctrine of St Thomas, who shall restrain him from much evil which he would otherwise do both to others and to himself. They perform the same office for all those who are hardened in sin, and their protection is not without many good results, even in the case of heretics and unbelievers. All these they serve as if they were their masters, although they are the slaves of hell, men who they perceive clearly will be damned, and who are walking in the high road of perdition.

Let us here stop and admire the goodness of the angels. Where is to be found the gardener who would water a tree if he knew that it would never bear fruit, and who would do it with as much care as if he had great expectations from it ? But how overwhelming is the thought, when we consider that they continue to prompt us to good with the same fidelity after having been repulsed thousands of times, and after having seen | the fruitlessness of their labour on a hundred thousand occasions.

All these affronts, all these insults, all this rebellion, all this perfidy, all this malice and atrocity of men, who are, so to say, engaged in a perpetual struggle with these glorious spirits, labouring to outdo their love with ingratitude, do not prevent them from being devoted to the service of all men. Let us weigh well these two great truths : all the nine choirs of angels, without a single exception, are in the service of men; and all men, however vile and wretched they may be, without a single exception are assisted by the angels. They go and seek them amidst the boundless forests of Canada, in the most distant wilds, and in the darkest dungeons, at the very ends of the earth, and in the centre of barbarism itself; and you would say that they were passionately enamoured of these men who have nothing human about them save the form, their life being altogether brutal—nay, far below that of beasts. These beings of heavenly beauty bestow their love on deformity itself, and receive in return nothing but insolent contempt. It is thus that these spirits love, who love only out of pure love, that is to say, who look only to God alone.

FIFTH MOTIVE.

The Holy Angels do all that is possible to be done for the Good of Men.

The angel who performed the office of a servant to that young man who is mentioned in the history of the Order of St Dominic, offers us a striking example of this truth. A pious lady was apprised late one evening that a poor woman who lived in one of the suburbs of the town where she was then residing, was in extreme want. All her servants being out, she sent her son, who was very young. But as the child was frightened at having to go in the dark to a quarter which was at some distance from his home, a page, who was passing before the door with a torch, conducted him to the woman's abode; and again, when he had to return, a man presented himself and escorted him back to his mother's house, who doubted not but that it must have been his good angel who had rendered him this charitable service. Truly it is much for angels to watch over men so lovingly, but to take their form and to appear visibly, as they have so often done, this is something greater still. And that learned commentator on Holy Scripture, Cornelius à Lapide, is of opinion, that after the resurrection they will at times assume forms of incredible beauty to gratify our external senses. But that which is still more wonderful, is to see them put themselves in every conceivable situation in order to serve us. They take the appearance of poor men, of beggars, of the sick, of lepers. There is nothing which they will not do for men, who scarcely do anything in acknowledgment of the benefits they receive from them.

Even were it only on certain occasions that they rendered this assistance to such vile and miserable creatures, it would be wonderful : but to confer benefits upon us as numerous as the very moments of our life, and after such a manner, this is indeed past all conception. We have said again and again that the angels are our guardians; you also who read this have often said it ; but have we ever seriously reflected on a favour so astonishing and so precious? If a prince of the blood royal were to repair to a wretched village, to pass some time in the service of a poor peasant, in a wretched hovel, would it not excite the wonder of the whole world? And if this peasant were his enemy, who constantly ill-treated him, and from whom the prince could expect nothing to his own advantage, doubtless this would much increase the general astonishment. And yet further, if this prince were not only to pass some months or even years with this wretched man, but were to remain with him to the latest moment of his life never losing sight of him, but always accompanying him, a man who was not only ungrateful to him, not only bad, but quite brutalised, covered with loathsome diseases, disgusting ulcers, vermin, itch, and everything that is most revolting, what would men think of this?

And yet, my soul, it is thus that thy good angel guards thee : it is thus, O thou to whom I speak through these pages, that thy holy angel guards thee, and affords thee his constant protection. Yes, this amiable prince of Paradise never leaves us in this valley of misery and tears. The angels, says St Augustine, go in and out with us, having their eyes always fixed upon us and upon all that we are doing. If we stop anywhere, they stop also; if we go forth to walk, they bear us company; if we journey into another country, they follow us ; go where we will, by land or by sea, they are ever with us. Let the solitary shut himself up in his hermitage, his good angel abides there with him ; let the traveller pass continually from one country to another, his good angel follows him everywhere. Oh, exceeding goodness! While we sleep, they keep watch by us ; they are always beside us,—us, who are sinners, and consequently their enemies ; who are hideousness itself by reason of sin, and who could not even endure ourselves if we knew our own deformity, and were sensible of our loathsomeness—us, who are ingratitude itself ; the greater part of whose lives is made up of criminal actions, either mortal or venial, or of mean and unworthy occupations, which assuredly are most pitiable in the eyes of those enlightened spirits, who plainly perceive their folly and vanity,—us, who mix a multitude of faults with the good actions we perform : and notwithstanding all this, they never tire of being with us all day long and all night long, and during every moment of our life. And if we are so happy as to be saved, after our death they will visit us in the prison of Purgatory, and will not think they degrade themselves by coming to console us amidst the furnaces and flames of that place of suffering. Truly, is not this to act as our servants and slaves, and not merely as our guardians? But, more than this: would it be possible—I do not say to meet with princes who should be willing thus to serve such miserable creatures—but could any persons be found, however wretched they might be, who would consent to serve kings on these conditions, and sacrifice their liberty to such a degree? Begin, then, to-day, truly to learn, and fix it well in your memory, that the angels are our servants and our slaves. Oh, the goodness of God ! Princes of Paradise, kings of glory, to be our attendants and our slaves ! That holy man, Vincent Caraffa, had indeed reason to say that the life of the Christian was something truly wondrous and admirable.

Add to this surprising love, that the angels are not satisfied with thus guarding men ; their love is carried to such an excess, that, for the love of men, they tend even beasts; not only in that sometimes, disguised as shepherds, they have watched over the flocks of certain chosen souls, as we read of St Felix,[1] who was afterwards a Capuchin, but that, according to St Augustine, the visible world is governed by invisible creatures, pure spirits; and that there are even angels who preside over every visible thing, and all the different species of creatures in the world, whether animate or inanimate. The heavens and the stars have their directing angels ; the waters have their own special angel, as is stated in the Apocalypse (xvi. 5); the air has its angels which govern the winds, as we may read in the same book (vii. 1), which, moreover, informs us (xiv. 18) that the element of fire also has its angels.* The kingdoms have their angels, as Daniel says (x. 13, 20); provinces also have their guardian angels, as we learn from Genesis (xxxii. 1) : for the angels who appeared to Jacob were the guardians of the provinces through which he was passing. Jacob, says St Augustine, saw two troops of angels ; one was commanded by the Angel of Mesopotamia, who had conducted that holy patriarch with his band to the confines of Canaan ; there that holy man was received by the Angel of Canaan, accompanied by a multitude of inferior angels, to serve him as an escort and defend him from his enemies.† Every country, in the opinion of St Clement, has an angel to guard it, and so have towns and villages, and even private families, in the judgment of the learned Tostado : how much more churches and altars, as it has pleased our Lord to reveal to several of His Saints.

Thus the whole world is full of angels; and this seems conformable to the sweetness with which Divine Providence orders things : for if it be true, as some aver, that there are in the air so great a number of devils that, if these spirits had bodies, they would cause the darkness of night at mid-day, hiding from us the sight of the sun, how should men, who are sheer weakness, be able to resist such might, if they were not succoured by the protection of the good angels ? Now, all these good angels are not stationed throughout this universe for no active purpose. As each star has its own peculiar influence, so likewise all these blessed spirits produce effects beneficial to men, after a manner proper to each; and if we did but know all the favours which we continually receive from them, we must have hearts harder than stone not to be sensibly affected by it. But, alas ! man is wholly given up to the flesh, and thinks of scarcely anything else but the objects with which his senses are conversant. It is vain to talk to him of spiritual things; either he comprehends them not, or he easily forgets them. Notwithstanding all that the Prophet Eliseus might say to his servant of the protection of these glorious spirits, the poor man did not feel any the more convinced of it, until God opened his eyes miraculously, and showed them to him under sensible forms. Oh, if the All-Good God were to grant to us the same favour, what wonders should we discover! However, let us well and deeply consider that all the comfort and benefit we derive from earth, air, water, fire, from the heavens, from animals—in fine, from all creatures, come to us by the agency of the holy angels, who are the faithful ministers of that only God whom we adore, who is admirable in all His gifts, and who merits for them our unceasing praises for ever and ever.

Notes

[1] St Felix of Cantalicio. a.d. 1587.

* See Note B.

† See Note C.

SIXTH MOTIVE.

The Holy Angels assist us in Temporal Things.

After having spoken of the benefits we receive from the angels in a general way, it is well to consider a little more in detail the favours they confer upon us, that the heart of man may be left without excuse, and be irresistibly constrained to love them. For if benefits, as says that holy man, Father Louis of Grenada, are to love what wood is to fire, which increases in intensity and magnitude in proportion to the fuel supplied to it, what fires and flames, what conflagrations, should not the love of the angels kindle in us, since on all sides we are loaded with their loving benefits? You would say that they were determined to bear away the palm of love, if you regard the considerate kindness with which they treat us, and the multiplied favours which they bestow upon us with unparalleled liberality and profusion. Let us consider this truth as respects temporal concerns; we will afterwards view it in regard to those spiritual benefits which help to bring us to a high and blessed eternity ; and we shall then be compelled to acknowledge that there is no good thing for which we are not indebted to the love of the angels.

The angels have care of our bodily nurture. It was by these glorious spirits that the infant St John the Baptist was brought up in the desert, whither his holy mother had taken him, to escape the persecution of Herod, and where she died forty days after her retreat into this solitude, leaving this blessed child, at the tender age of eighteen months, all alone in a wilderness, deprived of the assistance of any visible creature. They have a care also for our bodily sustenance. They carried to the Blessed Cléré Indoise,[1] in a rich vessel, manna whiter than snow, the taste of which was more delicious than the choicest earthly meats. They entertained the martyrs St Firmin and St Rusticus, and supplied them with abundant food. They carried a repast to Daniel in the den where he was confined (xiv. 32-38); and the holy prophet Elias, when he was lying on the ground so exhausted that there was no more strength in him, received at their hands food which imparted to him so much vigour that it was sufficient to enable him to walk during forty days, till he reached the holy mountain of Horeb (3 Kings xix. 5-8). They give drink to those who are thirsty. When Agar's child was at the point of death, they preserved his life by the water they pointed out to the afflicted mother (Gen. xxi. 14-19). They provide men with raiment : the virgin St Anthusa was arrayed magnificently by them. They confer honours upon them. A hundred angels appeared at the death of the blessed Agatha, and composed her epitaph. They promoted to the dignity of the episcopate the illustrious St Mello, Archbishop of Rouen; and exalted to the highest station on earth the Sovereign Pontiff, St Gregory the Great. They minister to the recreation of men, and afford them innocent pleasures. St Francis being sick, they played upon an instrument of music for his solace. They ministered the same gratification to St Nicholas of Tolentino, during the six months preceding his death. They caused the most ravishing music to be heard round the sacred body of the Mother of God during the space of three days, for the consolation of those who approached that divine tabernacle. They gave roses to St Rosaly in a desert where they bad never bloomed. They are forward to gratify the desires of their friends. St Agnes, of Monte Pulciano, wished for certain relics, and she received them accordingly at the hands of these amiable spirits. They procure temporal goods for those who serve them, when it is not contrary to God's appointment. It was by their holy devices that Jacob became rich, while he abode with his father-in law, Laban (Gen. xxxi. 11-13). They obtain children for married persons who are without them, as we read in the Book of Judges (xiii. 2-23), in the case of the wife of Manue. They make men eloquent, of which we have an instance in Isaias vi. 6-8. They make beautiful and rich presents : witness that magnificent picture which they gave to St Galla, a young Roman widow. They accompany travellers. We have a striking proof of this in the person of Tobias, who was conducted, with a goodness which perfectly enchants us, by St Raphael (Tob. v. 5, &c.). This same archangel, for three years, visibly accompanied St Macarius, the Roman, acting as his guide from the time he left Rome, whence this saint had fled on his marriage-day, until he had penetrated far into the desert. They visit and console the servants of God. AU the lives of the Fathers of the Desert are full of testimonies to this truth. St Ludwine was often visited by them, and the martyrs frequently received this honour in their prisons. But you must not suppose, says the learned Rupert, that they never visited them except in a visible form ; they were very near them even when they did not behold them, supporting them in the midst of their torments, giving them strength to bear their chains, and taking pleasure even in numbering all their wounds. It must have been an enrapturing sight to see them wiping away the sweat of a glorious martyr with a cloth of beautiful whiteness, and from time to time giving him water to drink, to minister some refreshment to him in his pains. O my God, O my God, how good it is to suffer something for Thee !

But if they procure all these good things for us during life, they also assist us and deliver us from all kinds of evil. They liberate from prison, break the chains of captives and set them at liberty, as Scripture records—(Acts xii. 7-11)—of the prince of the Apostles, and supreme head of the Church. They rescue from flames, as is related of Daniel (iii. 49); from conflagrations, as we read in Genesis (xix. 15-17); from lions, as we see in the case of the prophet just mentioned (Dan. vi. *22); from* calumny, infamy, and death, as the Holy Spirit declares to us of Susanna (xiii. 55, 59) ; from the sword, as we see in the person of Isaac (Gen. xx. 11). They heal men of every kind of malady, as St John, the beloved disciple, writes in his Gospel (v. 4). *We* learn in the fourth Book of Kings (i. 9-15), how they protect their friends, and are the adversaries of such as seek to injure them; they arm themselves on their behalf, assume the garb and form of soldiers, and go forth to do battle for them. *We* meet with marvellous examples of this in the Book of Machabees.[1] In fine, it would be necessary here to reckon up all the evils which can afflict us—whether in mind or body, or in our temporal, natural, and moral goods ; whether in regard to our private or our public interests; by wars, pestilences, or famines; whether by friends or foes—in order to specify all the various kinds of assistance we receive from the angels, and to teach all people that these are the gracious and powerful protectors, to whom we must have recourse in all our needs, whatever they may be. It is true, Divine Providence has given us the Saints for defenders; some against plague, as St Sebastian, St Roch, and St Adrian; others against toothache, as St Lawrence, and St Apollina ; others against disorders of the eyes, as St Clara, and St Lucy ; others in case of captivity, as St Leonard and St Paulinus. Thus, in the order of Providence, we have special recourse for one thing to one Saint, for another to another; but in the order of the same Providence the angels are appointed to assist us generally in all our distresses, and to obtain for us all sorts of good. We cannot do better than address ourselves to these loving spirits, and pay them private, or procure for them public devotions, to appease the auger of God, and draw down His mercies upon us.

Before concluding, let us here admire the protection of the angels in that admirable example given us in Scripture. It was an angel who led the people of God by that miraculous pillar spoken of in Exodus (xiii. 21, 22). It was one of these immortal spirits who communicated motion to that pillar which went before the people for the space of forty years, indicating to them the road they were to take in the midst of the desert, where there was no path to guide them. He made it move forward or stand still, according as it was necessary for the people either to journey onward or to rest. He caused it to be visible under the appearance of a cloud during the day, and under that of fire by night. He gave it its density, its width, and its height, that it might be easily discernible by so great a multitude, which, according to the opinion of the learned Pereyra, occupied ground to the extent of five leagues. By its means he provided them with a shade to protect them from the excessive heats of the sun. He caused it to leave its position in advance of the people and to pass to the rear, in order that, in this pillar, he might stand between the Hebrews and the army of Pharao, giving light to the former and blinding the unbelievers, whom he made to perish miserably in the waters of the Red Sea, which he divided for a brief space, that the people of God might walk through it dry-shod. The whole host of the Egyptians, numbering two hundred and fifty thousand armed men, was overwhelmed therein, not a single man remaining to tell the news. I leave it to the devotion of those who read of this wonderful guidance to meditate at leisure upon all its details. So striking are they, that it needs but a slight attention for us to be profoundly convinced that the services which the angels render to men are immeasurably great, and so be led to magnify the Holy Name of the Lord, who alone works all these wonders by the ministers of His heavenly court.

Notes

[1] The translator has been unable to discover who this holy woman was, or when and where she lived, although he has made inquiries in quarters which appeared to be most capable of furnishing the desired information.

[1] *E.g.*, 2 Mach. iii. 26, 26.

SEVENTH MOTIVE.

The Holy Angels render us great Services for Eternity.

Strictly speaking, there is but one only affair, which is the affair of affairs, the only great, the sole affair, and that is the affair of eternity. Everything which does not tend to that is nothing, and it is thus we must both think and speak of it. Oh, how contemptible, then, are the honours, the pleasures, and the goods of this perishable world ! Oh, how unworthy are all temporal matters to occupy a Christian soul ! Truly, truly, the whole world, and all that the world contains of what is sweetest or most afflicting, does not deserve that we should turn aside for one moment to look at it. How clearly shall we perceive these truths at the moment of our death, and how soon shall we thus behold them ! for soon shall we with astonishment perceive that the world exists for us no longer. Oh the folly of the human heart to allow itself to rest in it ! Would to God that this truth of Scripture might never depart from before our eyes : "The world passeth away, and the concupiscence thereof" (1 John ii. 17); and that we might once for all understand that that which passeth away ought to have no place in our hearts. Eternity alone ought to fill our minds; and the services we receive to help us to arrive there happily are the really great services which we ought to value. And here the love of the angels bears away the palm ; it is in this matter that they show themselves to be our true friends, and that the aid they render us is indeed inestimable.

These blessed spirits apply themselves with unimaginable zeal to procure for us the life of grace, which is the life of a glorious eternity. To accomplish this end they have been known lovingly to urge apostolic men to go and announce the Gospel to the people who were walking in the shadow of death, as appears in the case of St Paul and St Francis Xavier ; and with this design they have even been pleased to accompany those divine workmen who laboured to establish the life of eternity in souls ; as is related of St Martial, who had for associates in his apostolic functions twelve angels, who visibly assisted him. How many souls receive holy baptism through their charitable care, who, without their ministry, would have died in the death of original sin ! Father de Loret, of the Company of Jesus, relates a very remarkable example of this kind. In the month of January in the year 1634, in the city of Vienna, three souls delivered from Purgatory appeared to a religious of the same Company, to thank him because, through his prayers and mortifications, they were going to the enjoyment of eternal repose. "On the day of your birth," said they, "our good angels brought us the news of it, and promised us that you should one day be our deliverer, which consoled us much. Know, besides, that you are much indebted to your angel-guardian, because, had it not been for him, you would never have received baptism : the nurse had so tightened up your chest and throat, that you would have been suffocated if this loving guardian had not loosened the swaddling bands a little to enable you to breathe."

These amiable spirits are not satisfied with procuring for us that life of blessedness, but, like fond mothers, they take every possible care to preserve it to us, to maintain it, and to augment it. This is why they are so lovingly solicitous to procure for us the blessing of receiving the Adorable Body of our Good Master, who is the Life of our lives, and without whom we cannot have true life. How often have they carried this life-giving Sacrament of the Body of Jesus into deserts and other places, to preserve and increase the life of the souls to whom they gave It ! The blessed Stanislas, a novice in the Company of Jesus, of angelic purity, and himself a very angel upon earth, was honoured with these favours; and St Onuphrius furnishes in his own person an illustrious testimony to this truth. They neglect none of all the other means which may promote our eternal well-being. Prayer is one of the most certain and most profitable; and it is through their ministry that our prayers are offered before the throne of the Divine Majesty; indeed, amongst all the exercises of the spiritual life, there is none in which they are more present to assist us. Mortification is the twin sister of prayer; they should ever go together, and never be separated. What have not these holy spirits done, and what are they not continually doing, to engage us in the solid practice of this virtue, which is so necessary that without it nothing can be expected from a soul? for it is certain that to be truly Christian, we must be truly mortified. They have frequently appeared in a visible form to give holy lessons in this virtue, and their instructions have been worthy of the lights they possess.

It is also their holy occupation to inspire us with the love of all the other virtues, and particularly with the love of virginal purity, for it renders us like to themselves: it makes us their brethren, says St Cyprian; it unites us with them in a more intimate friendship. What have they not been known to do in its defence! They fight, they disguise themselves, they cause the death of those who assail it; they render invisible the persons who possess it, to deliver them from their peril; they change everything in nature for the preservation of a virtue which, raising man above human nature, causes him to lead upon earth a life all heavenly.

Their great care, however, is directed to inspiring us with love for Jesus and Mary, so worthy of all love. As they know that the love of these sacred Persons is the soul of all virtues, they bend all their endeavours to root it deeply in our hearts. St Dominic was one of the most fervent lovers of Jesus and Mary who ever lived, and he was also the well-beloved of the angels. He received at their hands all kinds of help during those long watches of the night which he spent prostrate at the foot of the holy altar, pouring forth the affections and longings of his heart without restraint in presence of his Good Master in the Most Holy Sacrament, and invoking with tears the protection of the Blessed Virgin. However wearied he might be while he was journeying on the road, he was never tired of watching whole nights in prayer, and used his utmost endeavours that it should be before the Adorable Eucharist. The angels, enraptured with this indefatigable love, associated themselves with him. These spirits of Heaven took pleasure in accompanying this heavenly man. They were seen to bring lights, and take them to the room into which he had retired, open first the doors of the house, and then of the church, whither they conducted him; and afterwards, when the time was come, they escorted him back in the same manner. The servants of a bishop with whom he lodged, having observed this marvel, mentioned it to the prelate, who watched the holy man about the time when the prodigy used to occur, and had the consolation of witnessing it, beholding with admiration the goodness of the heavenly spirits to men.

But because it is needful, in order to the practice of virtue, to have the mind enlightened and the will moved, they do not fail to communicate light to the understanding, and pious impulses to the heart; sometimes enlightening the understanding and moving the will by the manifestation of certain hidden truths under sensible similitudes; filling the mind with holy images which produce good thoughts; acting upon the external and internal senses ; stirring the spirits and humours of our bodies, and exciting desires in the sensitive appetite. They reveal the most divine mysteries of religion. It was through them that the Old Law was given, and that the greater truths of the New Law were manifested. The whole ancient dispensation is full of revelations made by the holy angels ; and under the new they announced to the glorious Mother of God the adorable mystery of the Incarnation; to the shepherds, the Birth of the Son of God; to St Joseph, the Conception of the Uncreated Word in the pure womb of his virginal spouse, and the place to which he was to conduct the Holy Child, in order to save Him from the persecution of Herod; to the Maries, the Resurrection of our Saviour ; to the disciples, His tremendous coming at the Last Judgment-day.

It is their constant thought, also, and unremitting care, to preserve us from sin, or to deliver us from it when we have fallen into it ; at one time by disclosures of Paradise, of Hell, or of Eternity ; at another, by the consideration of the fatal effects which follow crime; sometimes by piercing thoughts of death, and of the shortness of life ; and again, by the examples of saints, or by the punishment of sinners. Those lights, which sometimes in an instant open the eyes of the soul to the greatest truths, those sudden impressions, which surprise us when we least expect them, and which move us so efficaciously, come to us by the ministry of the good angels. There are happy moments when the heart feels itself strangely urged to give itself to God, without knowing why ; and that, too, in the midst of recreation, amusement, or festivity, on chance occasions, and even at the very time when we have resolved to commit some sin. It is the angels who produce these master-strokes of salvation, if we but know how to profit by them, obtaining for us from the mercy of God powerful graces, and on their part working wonders in our internal and external senses, moderating our passions, removing out of our way hindrances to the use of grace, overthrowing devils, and rendering easy to us all the means fitted to make us faithful to the attractions of the Spirit of God. They discover to us both our great and our little faults ; they show us our imperfections ; they manifest to us the most secret opposition which we offer to the Spirit of grace ; they dispose us to do penance, to make a good confession, to satisfy divine justice; and they have often assumed bodies to make themselves visible, that they might thereby converse with men on the affair of their salvation in a more sensible manner.

In fine, they animate and encourage us in arduous undertakings ; they comfort us in labours and sufferings ; they support us that we may persevere in virtue ; they obtain for us strength in mental distresses and scruples; they conduct us amidst the darkest paths; they revive our dejected spirits ; they fill us with joy, and procure for us that peace which surpasses all imagination, preserving the depth of the soul, amid all the storms and tempests which, in its own despite, agitate its inferior part, in a tranquillity which nothing can disturb. To these spirits it belongs to bestow joy and peace ; and so we see St Raphael saluting old Tobias with the words, "Joy be to thee always," and saying, "Peace be to you," on taking his leave (Tob. v. 11 ; xii 17). It is not the fault of the holy angels if peace reign not in the recesses of our souls ; but it is attachment to created things that hinders its sway. To remain ever at peace we must ever belong to God only.

EIGHTH MOTIVE.

The Protection of the Holy Angels against the Devils, with Particular Reference to their Different Temptations, which are here Treated of.

"Our whole life," says the devout St Bernard, "is nothing but one long temptation;" and this doctrine be bad drawn from Scripture, which teaches us the same truth—temptation without, temptation within, temptation on the part of our fellow-creatures, temptation arising from ourselves. It is a strange thing that we should be dangerous enemies to ourselves, that we should be obliged to be upon our guard and distrust ourselves, seeing that our destruction proceeds from ourselves, who often labour with our whole might to accomplish our own ruin. But we have also other battles to fight against enemies mighty in their strength, cruel in their fury, terrible in their cunning, countless in their multitude, indefatigable in their pursuit. Add to this, that they are pure spirits, who strike without being seen, who penetrate everywhere, who, though invisible, see all we do here below, and who contend with those who are excessively weak, and who walk in the midst of a dark night, on slippery paths, where it is almost impossible to keep from falling, and which are surrounded on all sides with frightful precipices, involving woes endless in their duration, and extreme in their intensity. Oh, if men did but meditate seriously upon these great truths, if they did but afford a little entrance to supernatural light, how thoroughly would they change their lives! Then truly would they serve the Lord with fear, and their flesh would be transfixed with dread of the frightful evils to which we are continually exposed, and to which, alas! we scarcely give a thought.

O you, whoever you may be, who read these things, read them not without giving them the greatest heed. These combats which yon are about to witness belong to a war which is not waged only against the kingdom in which you dwell, and the persons whom you love, it is against yourself that it is declared ; it is you whom these furious enemies attack ; it is with them you must fight ; it is over their strength and their cunning that you, who are nothing but sheer weakness and blindness, have to triumph, or you must be lost for ever. Repeat these terrible words : *Lost for ever ! lost for ever !* But, in good sooth, do we really know what we are saying when we use these words ? And if we know, why do we live like those who have never heard them?

Let us, then, place ourselves in presence of the Divine Majesty, and, after a hearty renunciation, for the love of God only, of all our sins, let us enter again into our interior. Having calmed all our passions, let us consider, in the tranquillity of our soul, that the devils are our infuriated enemies, who have all conspired our eternal ruin ; for they are so cruel in their rage that they are not only bent, like our earthly foes, on depriving us of our bodily life, which sooner or later we must lose, or on depriving us of our goods, our honour, and our friends, but it is our soul they plot against, to deprive it of an eternal kingdom, to rob it of a perfect joy and glory, and to plunge it into torments which the eye of man hath not seen, nor his ear heard, neither can his mind ever have conceived, and that for an eternity; that we may suffer inconceivable agonies in perpetual rage and despair, as long as God shall be God. This is why, in order to give us some faint notion of them, they are called in Scripture, wolves, lions, and dragons;[1] their cruelty surpassing the power of language to express.

This rage is accompanied with such strength, that we read in Job (xli. 24) that there is no power on earth which can be compared to it, and that the devil fears no one. All mankind united could not resist him without the special assistance of Heaven ; and millions of soldiers in battle array would be to this spirit like a little chaff which is scattered before the wind. Therefore it is that these angels of darkness are called in Scripture (Eph. vi. 12; ii. 2) "powers," and that they are styled princes and rulers of this corrupt world, the greater part of men being brought by sin into subjection to their detestable tyranny.

Add to their fury and strength a countless number of malicious artifices which they employ to seduce us, accompanied with such subtle and wicked inventions that the wisest have been deceived by them, and the most enlightened have been struck with blindness. This is why the apostle calls the devil "he that tempteth" (1 Thess. iii 5); and the name given him in the Gospel (Matt. iv. 3) is that of "the tempter." Again, he is styled in Scripture sometimes the dragon and the serpent, sometimes the hunter, a liar, and the father of lies, a spirit of error and of confusion.[1] The serpent, whose form he took, is the most subtle of beasts, as we read in Gen. iii. 1 ; and having deceived our first parents by his cunning, he has continued through the course of ages to tempt men by this means, finding it the best adapted to accomplish his end and to succeed in executing his most cruel designs. The lapse of ages only serves to render him more expert in deceit ; hence it is that later heresies are generally the most subtle. The temptations he employs become every day more dangerous; and this it is which may well make us tremble, seeing that while we become more feeble, our enemies become more formidable. "How," said the great Pachomius one day to him, "can you venture to assert that such and such things shall happen to my religious? Do you not full well know that the future is known to God alone, or to those to whom it pleases Him to reveal it ?" "True," answered the devil, "I do not know the future, but the great experience I have of things enables me to form such strong conjectures, that I often easily foresee them before they happen."

This, then, is an enemy whom men have had from the beginning of the world, and for six or seven thousand years he has never ceased to busy himself day and night in laying ambushes for them everywhere. St Anthony one day saw the world full of snares,—the air, the earth, the sea, and all the other waters. There are traps set for the eternal loss of souls in deserts and solitudes, in the midst of cities and assemblies, in palaces and castles, in the humblest cottages, alike in high and low estate; in pleasures and in sufferings, in riches and in poverty, in cloisters and in the world, in eating and drinking, in watching and sleeping, and in the holiest exercises. This enemy has darts and arrows ready prepared to let fly in all sorts of places and against all sorts of persons. He insinuates slander into men's discourse, and suggests impure thoughts in conversation between persons of a different sex; when anything is said which displeases us, he fails not at the moment to urge us to anger or revenge. He assumes every attitude, and takes every species of form. One while, as St Augustine remarks, he will take the shape of a wolf, and at another that of a lamb. Sometimes he will come and fight with us in the darkness, at others he will attack us at mid-day. There is a devil called in Scripture "the noon-day devil" (Ps. xc. 6).

He accommodates himself with wonderful tact to all our humours, studying our inclinations from our childhood. He notes the bent of our nature and that which is predominant in us : this is the point at which he especially directs his strongest battery, like the general of an army thoroughly experienced in the affairs of war, who assaults a city in the quarter where it is least defensible. He attacks us through our weakness ; he contrives a thousand opportunities of forming intimacies for those who are inclined to love; those who are of a sanguine temperament he excites to impurity and to indulgence in the pleasures of life ; the bilious to vengeance ; the melancholy to sadness, discouragement, and despair ; the choleric to quarrels ; the phlegmatic to sloth ; the timid to avarice ; while lofty natures he prompts to aspire to offices and dignities. He has in his snares baits suited to catch all kinds of persons, varying them according to the inclination of each, and the humour he perceives to be dominant at the moment.

In order the better to succeed, he shows only what is agreeable in honours and pleasures, cunningly hiding the evil in them, as the fisherman hides his hook in the bait he prepares for the fish. He hinders the sensual from reflecting on the shameful diseases, the dishonour and dissipation of substance, which attend upon impurity. He does the same with regard to all the other vices; he fills the imagination only with what pleases the humour, and diverts the eyes from the eternal wretchedness which is the great evil, the sovereign and only evil, lying hidden within this specious and deceitful good.

If he perceives that he gains nothing by one temptation, because at times the soul, by the help of grace, keeps special watch against it, he attacks it with several. He imitates those tyrants who, desiring to pervert Christians, and force them to renounce their holy faith, employed every variety of means to accomplish their purpose; sometimes proposing to them splendid alliances, wealthy marriages, the sweetness of this world's pleasures ; sometimes high offices and an exalted station. And when these generous martyrs were proof against all that could allure the senses, they endeavoured to overcome them by the fear of torments, and of everything most horrible. It is thus the devil makes war against men by all that can charm the senses or gratify the mind, and when he gains nothing in this way, he tries that of sufferings, whether external or internal. He assails us by means of sicknesses, loss of goods or of reputation, the desertion of friends, ill-treatment, contradictions, sadness, weariness, our own ill-humour, interior anguish, repugnances, scruples, and other great sufferings with which he afflicts us in relation both to God and men.

One of his chief objects is to choose his time well. Thus he will tempt a person strongly to impurity at a time when he is most inclined to it, and at the instant he remarks any violent excitement in the senses, or where the time, place, and person lend themselves to it, or on occasions when there is greater difficulty in resisting : as, for example, when a young girl, destitute of all protection, has her chastity assailed by offers of placing her in easy circumstances ; or he will incline persons to sin when they are less on their guard, or when they are in some part of the country where they are less provided with spiritual help, or on some day when prayer has been neglected, or other devotional exercises have not been attended to ; in a time of lukewarmness, or depression, or uneasiness, or discouragement, when some interval has elapsed since they were at confession and communion, or when they are deprived of sensible sweetness and consolations.

Sometimes these miserable spirits feign to retreat, like those generals who raise the siege of a town in order to retrace their steps, and take it when least expected. They will dissimulate for a length of time in order to make more sure of their blow. For example, you will see persons of a different sex, whether married or not, contract intimate friendships, entertaining at the time no bad intention, and years will sometimes elapse without either the one or the other thinking of evil. The devils do not tempt them, because, being persons who fear God, their intimacy would make them uneasy, if they perceived the danger of it; but when they see hearts deeply engaged, and familiarity established closely and confidently, then it is they put forth their power, and often with too fatal success. Thus they will allow persons to betake themselves to play, amusements, gay company, the reading of romances, good eating and drinking, and such like things, as balls, and parties of pleasure, where too much freedom is permitted; and in all this their object is to prevent souls perceiving that the spirit of devotion is growing slack within them. They will even preserve them from many faults which they might have committed on these occasions, in order that the habit may become so strong in them, that they may find a difficulty in freeing themselves, as they might easily have done at the beginning; and having thus caught them, they then begin to tempt them violently, and make them feel, only too late, the danger to which unknowingly they have exposed themselves.

They amuse with a false peace many who are living in vice or in error, causing them to give large alms, say many prayers, perform many mortifications, and such like works, deluding them with intellectual lights, sensible consolations, and an apparent tranquillity of conscience; and thus they deceive many who are in heresy, and who remain therein captivated by these fair semblances of virtue, which the devils also make use of even to attract those who were far removed from it : this is why heresies which assume the mask of piety are much more dangerous than those which are the offspring of unmixed licentiousness. I once knew a servant of God who was tormented with distressing temptations, and at the same time much inclined to embrace a heretical tenet, but as soon as he began to deliberate about adopting it, all his temptations used to leave him ; these spirits of hell employing this stratagem in order to persuade him that he might follow such opinion with a good conscience. It often happens that they have recourse to this artifice to stifle the remorse of those who have abandoned the Catholic faith, lulling their conscience to rest, and prompting them to the practice of many seemingly virtuous actions. They also employ it in the case of certain souls who, fearing to be lost eternally on account of some mortal sin in which they are entangled, try to quiet their self-reproach by good works, and thus to rid themselves, if possible, of their just fear of damnation.

These wretched spirits do their utmost to discover the designs of God with respect to a soul, with the view of misleading it in the ways of grace, and drawing it aside from its vocation. They will induce one who is called to serve the Church in the world, to enter the cloister, while, on the other hand, they will persuade him who is called to the cloister, to become a secular priest. If they observe that a person is called by grace to a wide sphere of action, and has a decided vocation to labour in various places for the good of souls, they will try to fix him in some cure, or prebend, or other benefice requiring residence. The holy man Avila, thoroughly penetrated with this truth, would never consent to the proposals made to him by a great prelate, with a view to detain him in his diocese; and the event proved plainly that the glory of God was interested in the matter. This consideration (independently of the particular reason affecting their Order) constrained several eminent members of the Company of Jesus, as is related in their history, to resist the urgent solicitations of the Emperor, who wished them to accept bishoprics. "Our labours," they said, "must not be confined to one diocese." "The whole world," said the late M. Vincent[1] to an ecclesiastic of great piety, who was refusing a cure of souls to which his uncle desired to present him, in order to enter the Congregation of the Mission—"The whole world must be your cure."

Others there are upon whom so general a grace has not been bestowed, and these they will induce to burden themselves with too many employments ; and thus, by exhausting their strength, they unfit them for the more limited duties which God requires of them. There are directors who have grace given them to conduct souls that are beginning to walk in the paths of virtue ; there are others who have grace to guide the more advanced ; there are others, again, who are endowed with admirable talents for directing those who are in the highest paths of perfection. It has been remarked that one of the most distinguished servants of God who has appeared in our age, was gifted with a marvellous grace for directing the most perfect souls, and very little, or scarcely any at all, for the conversion of sinners. Holy persons are also to be met with, whose labours in drawing souls out of sin are blessed with extraordinary fruit, but who have but little success in leading men on to eminent sanctity. It is a rare thing to meet with those who have a universal gift of direction : the devils, then, strive to divert the labours of directors from the line of their graces, and to make them undertake either too much or too little in the guidance of the souls which God sends to them. A great man of our day, very generally known by several volumes of Meditations which he published, said to a person who consulted him, "I have no knowledge of that way." And another religious of the same Congregation said, in answer to a person who asked his opinion concerning his state, "My lights extend only so far." These were souls truly devoted to God, who, notwithstanding the high esteem in which they were held, were not ashamed to acknowledge that there were certain states in the spiritual life into which they had no insight for the direction of others.

These artful spirits inspire those whom grace would lead to occupy themselves externally for the good of their neighbour, with a wish for solitude, and incline to an active life those whom grace would draw to retirement. "Oh, how many there are," says the holy man Avila, in one of his letters which we have already quoted, "who enter holy orders, and intrude themselves into the sacerdotal office, through the instigation of devils; who, seeing plainly their faults and vicious inclinations, know well the profanations and sacrileges which will hence result when such men have to celebrate the Holy Sacrifice of the Mass almost every day ! Many of these would have saved their souls in the married state.

They tempt fathers, mothers, and relatives, by the love of riches or honours, to compel their children, with a view to these objects, to enter into states to which God does not call them. Thus they will force them into the priesthood, or into religion, to relieve their family of the burden of their maintenance, or for the sake of aggrandisement; and from similar motives they will press them to accept some judicial appointment, though they do not possess the required knowledge, or the application necessary to acquit themselves worthily of the duties of a good judge or a good lawyer, or to fulfil the obligations of any other office which may be entrusted to them. Indeed we may say that the great majority of persons, through the arts of these wicked spirits, are altogether differently employed to what they ought to be.

If they cannot turn us aside from the paths of grace, they devise means to make us do things in a different manner to what God wills. Does God require of a soul fasting, watching, and the exercise of holy prayer, they will make it fast, watch, and pray too much. "This," says the devout Louis of Grenada, "is a common temptation with those who are beginning to serve God, and who often by these excesses render themselves unfit for the performance of what they ought to do, or might have been able to do in course of time. They contrive to conceal from persons the injury they are inflicting on mind and body, so that they may have more time to accomplish the ruin of both one and the other, persuading them that such practices do them no harm. God requires perfection ; they urge persons to pursue it with a natural eagerness which proceeds only from self-love. God desires us to feel sorrow for our faults ; they will mingle with it anxiety, despondency, melancholy, and vexation. God requires of us that we should labour for our sanctification with the help of His grace ; they will neglect nothing by which to move us to impatience, and dishearten us, proving to us, by the repeated faults into which we fall, that success is, so to say, impossible for us. They will do their utmost to make us either outrun grace, or lag behind it, prompting us to do things out of God's appointed season. We must do good, and we must do that good which God desires of us, in the manner which He desires, and at the time that He has ordained. St Philip Neri was undoubtedly called to the priesthood ; but it was God's design that he should not enter it until he was already somewhat advanced in years ; he therefore constantly resisted the solicitations of those who would have induced him to take holy orders before that time had come. The Adorable Jesus came into the world to sacrifice His divine life for its salvation ; and He flies and hides Himself until the time prescribed by His Eternal Father has arrived. "He hath put the times and the moments in His own power," said our gracious Saviour (Acts i. 7) ; it is not for us therefore either to hurry on before or to linger behind. Our dear Master was to die ; but He was to die at the time decreed by His Eternal Father. Silence is a great virtue, nevertheless St Francis reproved one of his religious because he carried it to excess.

God demands of souls the exercise of holy prayer. The devils will detain at discursive prayer, or at simple meditation, those whom the Holy Spirit is attracting to divine contemplation ; while they will raise others to contemplation who ought still to proceed by the discursive way. They will encourage souls to proceed from active to passive contemplation whom the Spirit of God does not lead thereto; while to those whom He has so led, they will suggest fears, and cause others to suggest them. They will give sensible consolations, to draw men away from resting on pure faith, or to enfeeble their bodily powers ; they will impel to too much application of the imagination and the understanding, and try to injure the brain. They will transform themselves into "angels of light," [1] by false visions, revelations, interior utterances; and their stratagems are so artful, that they will even make their operation pass for purely intellectual visions—an operation so subtle, that it would seem as if the external and internal senses had no share in it, and that it was consequently a supernatural operation of the Spirit of God ; and this that men may put their trust in it, and thereby fall more deeply into delusion.

God wishes us to go to confession : they will make us approach this sacrament from self-love, in order to be relieved as soon as possible of the burden of our sins ; not so much from the love of God, and the movement of His grace, as from the love of ourselves, because our pride is hurt by seeing itself in so humiliating a condition. It is also observable that such as approach in this manner fall more grievously afterwards. We may confess every day, nay, frequently during the day, as some Saints have done ; but then we must do it as they did it.

God requires us to go to communion : the devils will hinder the frequentation of this Sacrament of Love, or they will induce souls to approach it too often who have not the necessary dispositions, and even at times are prompted by a secret movement of self-love, though they do not perceive it. A student, a regent, a preacher, a judge, a bishop, ought to attend to their respective avocations, and fulfil the duties of their state : the devils, under the pretext of retirement, disengagement from the world, or application to prayer, will make them quit their studies, their professional employments, or the care of their diocese ; and, on the other hand, under the plea of study, business, or the onerous cares which the Episcopate imposes, they will induce them to throw themselves entirely into external occupations, and the prelate, the judge, the preacher, will do nothing but study, talk of business, and mix with the world, without scarcely allowing time for prayer and converse with God.

O my God ! to what a miserable state is the human heart reduced through the artifices of these ministers of hell, even in the highest paths of grace ! The Venerable Father John of the Cross,[1] a man of eminent sanctity, teaches us that even in those who are aspiring to perfection there is to be found a certain secret satisfaction in their own good works, a wish to give others lessons in the spiritual life, an itching desire to talk about it. The devils, says this great master of the way of perfection, prompt them to perform many of their good works from a motive of self-love. Sometimes they manifest their devotion by exterior demonstrations, such as gestures or sighs, and are too ready to talk of their virtues, though even in the confessional it is with difficulty they can get themselves to make a simple declaration of their faults. At times they make little account of their sins ; at others they grieve for them to excess. They are reluctant to praise others, and are too glad to be praised themselves. They are never satisfied with the gifts and graces of God, or with the counsels and directions they receive, or the books they read. They take up curious practices of devotion. When they do not enjoy sensible sweetness in prayer, they are angry with themselves and with others. They declaim against the vices of others with an intemperate zeal, and rebuke them in the same impatient spirit. They would wish to become saints in a day, and their desires of perfection are so purely natural and so imperfect, that the more good resolutions they make the more faults they commit. They seek after sensible pleasure in their devotional exercises, and take to practising excessive austerities, which they sometimes conceal from their directors ; or, again, they will argue with their spiritual fathers, and try to bring them over to their views. They relax their endeavours, and give way to sadness, when contradicted, and believe that all is going ill with them when they are denied their little practices of devotion. They think the ways by which they are being led are not understood, when any opposition is made to their views. They would have God do their will ; hence they readily believe that what is not to their taste is not according to the will of God. They envy the spiritual good of their neighbour, and are troubled when they see themselves outstripped in the ways of grace. In fine, they have no love for the cross and pure mortification, for complete abnegation and annihilation of self.

Not but that the devils sometimes avail themselves of sufferings, tempting souls who they foresee will not make a good use of them to long for crosses ; or urging them to take them upon themselves, because, not being of God's disposal, they will easily sink under the weight of them ; or, again, they will induce them to augment such crosses as come to them in the order of God's providence. For instance, God sends some mental suffering which ought to be borne with patience and resignation : they will induce the persons thus afflicted to contemplate their sufferings, to reflect too much upon them, and thus to aggravate their own misery. As they throw a veil over the evil which resides in unlawful pleasures, so they conceal from men the good which sufferings contain ; they allow men to perceive only what is painful in them, for the purpose of tempting them to impatience, weariness, despair, and murmuring against the leadings of God's providence. They exert all their powers to cast souls into a state of despondency, leading them to regard their evils as irremediable, and to look only at this present life, and so urging them to desperation. They even harass souls with painful temptations with respect to God, tormenting them with suggestions against faith, or with fears of their own reprobation, or with doubts as to whether they have consented to sin ; confusing the imagination and leaving the mind disquieted, from uncertainty as to whether consent has been given to the temptation or not ; raising in people's consciences scruples with regard to their confessions, which they fancy they have never properly made ; persuading persons to make fresh general confessions unadvisedly, and often to repeat their ordinary ones through fear of not having mentioned everything, or of not having been sufficiently explicit, thus keeping the soul in a state of anguish for, as these spirits are themselves devoid of all hope, and in a perpetual state of unrest and unutterable disquietude, the effects they produce are akin to their own wretched condition. Wherever they approach they cause trouble, despondency, sadness, and confusion; and, if they cannot make men the companions of their misery hereafter, they endeavour at least to make them share their wretchedness in the present life ; and again, they harass us with contradictions from without, exciting our relations, our friends, and such as are under obligations to us, to provoke us, as we see in the case of Job's wife, at the same time representing to our imagination their ingratitude and injustice.

Sometimes, by God's permission, they take possession of the imagination of good people, even to such a degree as to make them see things quite differently to what they really are, thus rendering unavailing everything that can be said or done to undeceive them. That holy man, Father John of the Cross, was imprisoned by the religious of his Order, and strangely ill-treated ; he was even stripped of his religious habit, as one who was incorrigible. Men wonder at seeing so great a servant of God treated after this manner by good men, but we have no reason to be surprised : God, designing to make him a man of suffering, permitted the devil to try him cruelly ; and to this end these lying spirits made the religious who tormented him look upon him only as a disobedient person, who was wanting in the spirit of submission ; and there seemed to be some ground for this opinion : for in a Chapter of the Order which had been held, several distinguished religious, men high in authority, and considerable for their learning and personal merits, had decided that Father John of the Cross should not proceed any further with the matter begun : thus he was regarded as a rebel. People did not fail to say that his designs, however good they might be, ought to be abandoned, since he had been forbidden to think any longer of them; that, moreover, he was a person devoid of discretion, calculated only to attract public attention, and create much confusion in the Carmelite Order, by reason of his imprudent and head-long zeal. No attention was paid to anything alleged on the contrary part; and this, indeed, was clearly apparent in the last persecution to which he was subjected on his death-bed from the Prior of the house where he, lay sick. This Prior, though one of the reformed religious, and that too at the beginning of as holy a reform as ever took place, at a time also when the first-fruits of the renewed perfection of this holy Order were most rich and abundant, put an evil interpretation on all the actions of the man of God, and became thereby to him the cause of the severest trials. It is wonderful to find his Provincial visiting this monastery, and doing all in his power, both by his authority and by argument, to soften the mind of the Prior, yet in vain: the devil who possessed his imagination kept it filled with illusions which made him see things quite otherwise than what they were. At last, some little time before the man of God expired, the devil having withdrawn, the superior was seized with a sudden astonishment at what he had done: yet nothing new had occurred, all was as before, only the devil had departed.

The smallest imperfections give great advantage to these apostate spirits. The slightest things, as it is truly observed in the Life of St John Chrysostom, lately published, suffice to furnish them with an occasion for exciting violent passions against those who are combating them by labouring to restore primitive strictness of life and manners. These princes of darkness avail themselves of the most trifling acts of a faithful servant of God to provoke and foment a fierce opposition against him, blackening things the most innocent. In the days of persecution, bishops and priests died in defence of the faith; but now that the Church is in peace, bishops and priests can no longer be persecuted save for maintaining strictness of discipline. The devils do for the imagination what certain mirrors do for the eyes: they magnify appearances, and can make atoms look like high mountains.

They make things seem, as we have said, quite different to what they truly are, like those glasses which change the colour of the objects seen through them. They present very false notions of true devotion, making it appear to consist in what it does not,—that is to say, in particular practices, inward lights and sensible movements ; and making it not to appear where it really is,—that is to say, in a firm resolve to do the will of God in all things, and in the manner He wills. They persuade men of the world that devotion is fitted only for the cloister, and represent it in such a light as to make it seem impossible for them to practise it. All their artifices tend to make it look unattainable to persons living in the world, that they may put the very thought of it out of their minds; or they represent it under so frightful an aspect that they have not the courage to embrace it ; or they impute to it the defects of those who profess it, in order to decry it.

As their own nature is all malice, they insinuate a malicious tendency into the minds of men, making them see something evil in the most holy actions, and indining them to put a bad interpretation on the acts of others : all which is the very opposite to true charity, which thinks well of every one, and when it cannot approve the action, at least excuses the intention. It is one of the commonest faults in the world to be slow to believe what is good, and ready to think what is evil. If we can find nothing to blame in a life, the virtuous tenor of which looks like a reproach to ourselves, we direct our attacks against the interior, and, invading the very recesses of the heart, which is known to God only, we charge it with hypocrisy and dissimulation St Teresa relates that the Holy Lady of Cardona spoke readily of her graces, and was very frank in mentioning her virtues, and she regards this conduct as that of a soul who looked to God alone, without considering self : another would have condemned it as proceeding from vanity, and would have suspected this virtuous lady of seeking the esteem of creatures.

Father Caussin, in his "Holy Court," reflecting upon this truth, that we ought to be very cautious in passing judgment upon the actions of our neighbour, after having highly extolled the conduct of the great St Francis de Sales, remarks, that a critical spirit would have seen much in it at which it might take exception. For instance, says this eloquent author, the Saint testifies that the recollection of Madame de Chantal, of glorious memory, is so dear to him, that he often recurs to it, and thinks of her with affection, and that even at the holy altar. A censorious spirit might be scandalised at the imagination of a holy man being thus occupied with the remembrance of a woman; and yet in him it was a movement of grace. On the other hand, we read of saints who begged of God that they might never remember, even in their prayers, the women who had recommended themselves to them. Their particular grace led them to act thus; but the ways of the Holy Spirit of God in the conduct of His saints differ so widely that they are an inscrutable abyss to poor human reason.

When the devils foresee that great spiritual assistance is preparing for souls, or that special benedictions are about to be showered on a city, a diocese, or a province, they raise fierce persecutions against those whom God designs to employ for this purpose; they use every means to calumniate them, and to inspire people with a horror of them; and not only do they assail those who are employed in public ministrations, but they persecute such as lead the most retired and solitary life, when they observe in them any extraordinary virtue; for, says St Teresa, these souls never go alone to heaven—they save and sanctify a great number of persons by their prayers and by their union with God. We have seen in our days a religious of the Discalciated Carmelites leading a most solitary life on Mount Carmel, imitating those ancient Fathers who retired into the wildest deserts, that he might spend some time in complete separation from the society of men. The rage of the devils against this servant of God is something quite marvellous to read of.

If they apprehend that the genuine piety of some chosen soul, and the extraordinary graces with which Heaven has endowed it, will be productive of much fruit in the Church, they will labour to put some deluded creature forward, making this miserable being pass for a saint, and then they will expose the delusion, in order to lead men to the conclusion that they who are truly moved by the Spirit of God are deceivers likewise, and thus hinder the good which they might have effected. If they see devotion taking firm root in a country, through the solid practice of the frequent use of the sacraments, the exercise of prayer and union with God, they will cause some of those who make profession of devotion to fall into certain faults, and they will then raise a cry against frequent communion, against prayer, and other exercises of piety ; they will throw ridicule on the devout, and exert their power to the utmost to oppose the designs of God. O my Lord ! exclaims the seraphic Teresa, how does it move one to pity ! If a soul is deceived in the ways of prayer, people exclaim and raise a great outcry, and men do not perceive that for one who goes astray from praying amiss, thousands of souls are lost from the neglect of prayer. The pious Louis of Grenada, in his "Memorial," devotes a chapter to showing that it is often a great mistake to cry out so much against the abuse of frequent communion ; not but that we should condemn such abuse, and have a horror of it ; but we fail to observe, says this learned master of the spiritual life, that, under the pretext of some abuses which occur, we not only hinder the great progress of holy souls in virtue, by the frequent use of communion, but also, which is of the highest importance, much glory which would redound to God. Our Lord revealed to St Gertrude that those who prevented frequent communion, robbed Him of His delight. St Thomas teaches that daily communion was matter of precept in the first centuries. The holy Council of Trent expresses a wish for the restoration of this practice. It is the duty of confessors to examine the state of those who receive holy communion every day, that they may not make a bad use of it; but to disapprove a practice which was so habitual in the primitive Church, and which the last General Council desired, if possible, to restore, can but proceed from the hatred which the spirits of hell have conceived against this Mystery of Love.

A great servant of God has wisely observed, that there are certain persons in whom the devils seem to entrench themselves as in a fortress, and by whose means they render their temptations the more dangerous. There are persons whose very presence disposes to impurity, while there are others who inspire feelings of revenge, or again, of vanity. The devils lodge themselves in the eyes of some; in their hair, in their hands, and make everything about them fascinating—their voice, their words, the expression of their eyes, their gestures—so that it is difficult not to be seduced by them. People are sometimes surprised at seeing miserable men attach themselves to very ordinary women, deserting for them wives who are both beautiful and pleasing. This often happens through the secret artifices of the devils, who invest wretched beings, who naturally ought to inspire aversion, with a charm to ensnare hearts. A sick man at the point of death was in a state of great peace; one of his friends, a heretic, entered his room to pay him a visit; at the same moment he felt himself greatly tempted against the faith. The devils, who had no vantage-ground from whence to attack this poor sick man, found in this heretic a fortress, as it were, from which to direct their assaults upon him. I was told this by the late M. Le Gauffre, the worthy successor of Father Bernard, of glorious memory; and the circumstance is well worthy of notice, that we may take heed what company we keep, and not give place to the devils to tempt us, particularly at the hour of death. Let us here observe, that as the devils make violent assaults upon us by means of those who are in their power, so also the Spirit of God gives us great assistance by means of those souls which He fills with His presence. The blessed Angela of Foligni, when performing some journey of devotion, was favoured with extraordinary gifts; and our gracious Saviour revealed to her, that if she had chosen any other companion than the one who travelled with her, who was a person of much virtue, she would have been deprived of all these graces. Nothing is more pernicious than conversation with the wicked, nothing more profitable than intercourse with the good.

In fine, the great havoc which these accursed spirits make is by the establishment of heresy. For this end they have recourse to all their artifices; beginning with things which at first are not calculated to excite so much alarm. They instigated Luther to cry out against Indulgences ; but they made him commence by declaiming against the abuse of Indulgences and of ceremonies, and then by degrees they got at the faith.

St Teresa taught that great courage is required in spiritual warfare ; and this is very true, since our enemies are not only terrible in their strength, cruel in their rage, and inconceivably formidable in their stratagems, but they are indefatigable in pursuit ; they are ever lying in wait to surprise us; they watch for our destruction while we sleep. "Our enemies," says St Augustine, "are ever on the alert to work our ruin, and we are ever forgetful of our salvation." They watch without ceasing to make us die an eternal death, and we are ever slumbering when our very salvation is at stake. The necessities of eating and sleeping, and other bodily cares with which we are burdened, never diminish their activity, seeing that they share them not. They are always under arms day and night, and during the whole course of our life, never laying them down. If they appear occasionally to leave us at peace, or to grant a short truce, it is only that they may fight against us at more advantage, and renew the combat with greater violence and more success.

Moreover, they are pure spirits, as swift as thought, penetrating everywhere, pursuing us everywhere; nothing remains closed against them. In vain may you shut and bar your doors, and lock your rooms and your closets, ingress is still as free to them ; and as they are invisible, they assail you unperceived ; they strike, and you behold no one; they are beside you meditating your ruin, and you know it not ; their weapons are invisible : hence you may judge how difficult it is to defend ourselves against them. All this time they tempt us ; and Cassian tells us that the Fathers of the Desert knew by experience that they were most strongly tempted at the most holy times, as, for example, during the holy season of Lent.

These attacks become more violent in proportion as our love of God increases. From the moment we begin to serve Him, we must prepare for temptation. Nor ought this to astonish us, for now it is that war is openly declared ; hitherto they had given themselves little trouble, for the soul was already their slave. The saints often find themselves on the very edge of the precipice, through the violence of their temptations. It is the saints, says Cassian, who are often the most tempted by the desires of the flesh. That infernal Pharao loads with burdens those who endeavour to escape from his cruel thraldom. There is no spot on earth where we are exempt from this warfare. Our very churches, and the most holy places, do not preserve us from it ; they insinuate themselves everywhere. In solitude they caused poor Loth to fall into impurity, who had preserved himself chaste in the midst of a town wholly filled with monstrous licentiousness. There is no period of life which protects us from their assaults. An eminent and holy solitary, who resisted their temptations in his youth, choosing rather to allow his body to be burned in material fire than to abandon his soul to the fire of impurity, and thus had successfully withstood the shameless assault of a woman who laid snares for his virtue, allowed himself, at the age of sixty, to be vanquished by his tempters, through the instrumentality of a woman possessed by them. Let us pause briefly to consider this example, and let us tremble as we do so. A young man, who in the flower of his age had won such glorious triumphs, permits himself to be conquered, and that in old age, after so much fasting and mortification, with a body consumed by great austerities : after so many victories achieved during a long course of years, after a heavenly life, so many extraordinary gifts, so many miraculous graces, he allows himself to be overcome by a woman who was possessed, which in itself should have filled him with horror ; and that, too, after having expelled the devil out of her body.

One of their endeavours is to weary us by the length of the contest ; and experience sufficiently attests that men will give way at last, after having resisted a long time. A soul will persevere faithfully in its exercises, in spite of all the disgust and repugnance with which it may perform them, although it experiences no sensible feeling of devotion, and goes through them laboriously and painfully ; and at last it will suddenly be overcome with weariness, and will yield to the temptation. It will submit itself to the good advice given to it, and will observe with inviolable fidelity the commands laid upon it ; yet in the end it will follow its own devices, and give itself up to its own notions and inclinations. When these wretched spirits perceive that they can obtain no advantage, they go for reinforcements ; they take with them other demons, still more powerful and malicious, and, returning to the charge, often succeed in vanquishing those who had previously triumphed over them.

Besides all this, their number is beyond conception. St Bernard says that the devils, who are the apes of the Divinity, make a division of their forces, so that every man may have a bad angel, even as he has a good one. St Gregory of Nyssa is of the same opinion. St Anthony often said that millions of devils roamed over the earth. St Hilarion, his disciple, asserted the same thing, and referred, in confirmation of it, to the Gospel history, whence we learn that one single man was possessed by a "legion" of them, that is to say, by six thousand six hundred and sixty-six. The glorious St Dominic delivered an unhappy man from fifteen thousand devils, who had entered his body in punishment for the scoffs he had uttered against the fifteen mysteries of the Rosary. This is well worthy of the consideration of those who sneer at associations established by lawful authority; but anyhow let us reflect what a host of enemies are banded together for the ruin of one single man. St Jerome, commenting on the sixth chapter of the Epistle to the Ephesians, declares that it is the general opinion of theologians that the air is filled with these invisible enemies.

Now if this be so, let us consider with a little attention the dangers to which we are exposed, having such enemies to contend with ; and let us at the same time reflect what we ourselves are, who have to fight against such forces. We live in the midst of darkness, and even in the full daylight of grace we fail to see, being blinded by our passions. We walk in places where eternal precipices abound, and upon paths so slippery, that the holiest find it a hard matter to keep from falling ; we are ignorant of the road we should take, and, as St Bernard says, we readily choose that which leads to hell ; they whom we meet are as blind and ignorant as we are, and, instead of aiding to bring us out of our false ways, serve only to lead us on therein to our ruin. In ourselves we are weakness itself, pierced on all sides with mortal wounds. O my God ! O my God ! in such a deplorable condition, who shall escape ? Alas ! O men, what are we thinking of when we live in forgetfulness of these frightful perils ? Is it, then, possible that these truths should be indubitable, and yet that we should give them so little serious reflection ? Surely a spell must be upon us, that, having eyes, we see not, having ears, we hear not, and having feet, we yet remain motionless, when Eternity is at stake : we see, we hear, we move only for this present life.

It is because of this blindness and insensibility that the greater part of men become the prey of devils. If we would but let ourselves be guided by the light and movements of grace, unable as we are to do anything of ourselves, we could do all things in Him who is our strength.[1] It is in His might that we must courageously resist the power of the devils, who, like to crocodiles, fly from those who pursue them, and pursue those who fly from them. "Resist the devil," so teaches the Divine Word (Jas. iv. 7), "and he will fly from you." It is true that our strength is altogether unevenly matched with his, but the power of Jesus Christ supplies for our weakness. The great St Anthony affirmed, that since the coming of Christ we may vanquish the devil as we would a sparrow, and break his power as if it were so much straw.

We must place all our confidence, then, in Jesus Christ and His holy Cross, and in the protection of His Blessed Mother, who has crushed the head of this wretched serpent; and we must make use of the sacraments, of holy water, of holy images, to bring to nought all his efforts, keeping ourselves always, on the other hand, in the practice of humility, a virtue which is all-powerful to frustrate the temptations of hell, but without which all the other virtues will avail but little against its assaults. St Anthony, of whom I have just spoken, when he had a vision of the world filled with snares, and saw a devil, whose head touched the stars, carrying off the greater part of souls as his prey, was penetrated with grief, and, crying out aloud, the holy man exclaimed, "Who, then, shall be able to escape these traps, and from the hands of this infernal monster?" To which a voice from heaven replied, "Anthony, humility shall do this." This virtue must be accompanied with an entire distrust of ourselves. If we put any confidence in our own strength, in our experience, our discretion, our resolutions, we are lost; sooner or later we shall infallibly perish : and we must be greatly on our guard against a secret self-reliance, which is sometimes imperceptible to ourselves; it appears to us that when we have gone through certain devotional exercises the victory is gained, and then our Lord permits us to fall grievously.

There are some souls who see clearly enough certain imperfections, which they detest; they groan, they strive, and yet they cannot conquer them : this is, said that holy man, Father de Condren, because these souls have not as yet thoroughly learned their weakness, their insufficiency, their helplessness. Mistrust in ourselves ought to be followed by fear. "Fear the Lord," it is written (Ps. xxxiii. 10), "all ye His saints." If the saints must work out their salvation with trembling, what ought sinners to do? One thief near the Cross is saved; another equally near is lost. God pardons one of His disciples who denied Him; He condemns another who betrayed Him. There is a Heaven, but there is also a Hell. Some have truly repented at the hour of death; thousands and thousands have died in sin. In fine, the most brilliant lights of the Church have been seen to suffer an eclipse ; men who were as angels upon earth have, at the last moment of their life, precipitated themselves into hell by a movement of pride ; pillars of the Church have been shaken and overthrown ; they who had brought to others the pure light of faith have fallen into heresy; saints have become devils.

For this cause we should stand strictly on our guard, and give no place to temptation, by avoiding all those occasions which might lead us into it. "Watch and pray," says the Divine Word (Matt. xxvi. 41), "lest you enter into temptation." It does not say lest temptation enter into you, but lest you enter into temptation. When it is by God's dispensation that we find ourselves in peril, we shall, by the help of His divine assistance, escape ; but if it is of our own seeking that we are involved in it, we shall perish. Joseph's temptation was far stronger than that of David : Joseph was young, David was old; Joseph was pursued by the caresses and threats of a woman who importuned him incessantly, David was pursued by no one. The chastity of Joseph was assaulted by a woman who was his mistress; by resisting her he ran the risk of his life ; by giving the reins to passion he might attain to a great temporal fortune. David was a king ; he had nothing to fear and nothing to expect, save the remorses of his conscience. David was more advanced in the spiritual life, and he was the man according to God's own heart. Nevertheless, David was vanquished by temptation, and Joseph resisted ; and this was because David exposed himself to the temptation, while Joseph met with the danger while acquitting himself of his duty in the order of God's providence. The Three Children were delivered from the furnace of Babylon, and Peter from the peril of the waters; but should you throw yourself into fire or into water, you would be burned or drowned. If you are of a bilious temperament, why do you not shun the occasions of anger ? If you feel disposed to love, why do you not discreetly avoid the company of women? You lose your temper at play, why then do you not renounce gaming ? You are full of distractions when you pray in places not sufficiently retired, why then do you not choose such as are more appropriate ? St Ignatius, the founder of the Company of Jesus, was favoured with the privilege of suffering no distractions in time of prayer ; but it behoved him, on his part, to do what in him lay. When he failed to withdraw himself far enough from the world and from its noise, he no longer enjoyed this grace.

Be prompt also in resisting temptation. The same saint said that the serpent easily draws in his body where he has insinuated his head. The negligence with which you resist temptation gives great hold to your enemies. They greatly fear those souls who resist their attacks from the very first, because they perceive that these attacks serve but to win crowns for them. If a burning coal were to fall on your dress, would you not instantaneously, and with the greatest expedition possible, shake it off on the ground ? and however short a time you might allow it to rest on your clothes, would they not be injured by it ? Although the negligence may not be fully voluntary, from the advertence of the mind not being entire, it is still a venial sin ; and one single venial sin gives a strange power to the devil to tempt us. When the exorcists of the possessed at Marseilles had committed the most trifling little fault, they were powerless against the devils for some time. On the other hand, when we have promptly repulsed temptation the devils are afraid of returning, and their strength is weakened. We must never deliberate : a town which parleys is all but taken. The very moment we perceive the sin, or the occasion of sin, we must break off, we must go away; we must suffer anything rather than dwell upon it.

In combats where chastity is concerned we must conquer by flight. Do not stay considering the temptation; fly as fast as you can. Temptations against purity have charms for the senses, which catch you if you look at them. In temptations against faith we must never reason; "we must fly," said St Francis de Sales, "by the door of the will, and not by that of the understanding. Beware of going in search of arguments to conquer these sorts of temptations. Dispute not with the devil, he is too clever for you ; you will never disentangle yourself from the difficulties he will present." The holy Bishop whom we have just quoted relates that this spirit of subtilty and malice suggested to him so powerful an objection against the Presence of our Lord in the Eucharist, that, without a special succour of grace, he had been lost. This is why this incomparable prelate would never mention what the difficulty was which formed the matter of his temptation, for fear it might cause the loss of some soul.

In other interior sufferings we must abandon ourselves entirely to God, and avoid all voluntary reflection upon them. We cannot prevent the imagination from being assailed by them; but we ought to bear them with patience, and not minister to or aggravate them by willingly dwelling on them. They usually incline persons to reverie, and this they should avoid, occupying themselves in some quiet way, that they may give the least possible place to them. An exaggerated apprehension of them imprints their images more strongly on the mind, and, in the case of temptations to impurity, the senses are consequently more excited.

In sufferings arising from scruples or other disquietudes, the remedy is, not to abide by your own judgment, but to take advice of some person of experience in these ways (for there are eminent directors who have no knowledge of them), one also who is learned and gifted with decision, and to refer the matter to his opinion, whether it be question of not reiterating general confessions, although you may yourself believe you have need of so doing, or of not continuing to accuse yourself of certain faults or doubts; for, after all, the order which God has established in

His Church is that we should be directed, not immediately by Himself, but by means of those whom He has called to the sacred functions of the priesthood. A person who, acting against his conscience, should commit a sin which he judged to be mortal, although in fact it was only a venial fault, would doubtless, supposing he acted with full deliberation, be guilty of a grievous sin; but if, notwithstanding his own opinion of the enormity of the fault, he should put it aside, out of submission to the judgment of his director, who is more enlightened and better skilled to discriminate between sin and sin, he would assuredly be right in so doing. But, you will say, he is going against his conscience. True, but then it is a conscience in error, and he follows the rules of a conscience rightly informed, that of the director. Neither should we trouble ourselves because the idea occurs to us that we have not explained ourselves with sufficient clearness, or that the director does not fully understand our state (temptations common to almost all who suffer in this way), nor perplex ourselves as to whether our sufferings are the consequence of our sins ; for, after having renounced our faults, it is expedient that we should bear the penalty of them in peace. The pains of Purgatory are certainly the penalties and chastisements of sin ; but does this prevent the souls subjected to them from bearing them with tranquillity, and a perfect resignation to the decrees of God ?

In sufferings from temptations to blasphemy or the idea of reprobation, we ought quietly to avoid voluntary reflections thereon ; and at these times a general consideration of our Lord is more advisable in prayer than a special meditation upon the mysteries, because the temptation is maintained and increased by a distinct consideration of the truths of faith. Above all, we must be careful not to give way to discouragement, whatever faults we may commit Were you to fall a hundred times in the course of a day you must rise again a hundred times. Would it not be absurd in a man to remain lying in the middle of a street, in the mire and dirt, because he had happened to fall down several times? Let us indeed humble ourselves for our faults, and feel regret on account of them, but never let us be discouraged by them. This is a universal maxim: weariness and impatience are the cause of much evil. Let us learn to bear with ourselves in our defects, waiting with patience for the Lord to help us. Too much eagerness to attain perfection is a hurtful temptation, for we often desire it from self-love. Our pride makes us wish to see ourselves speedily perfect, and leads us to be astonished when we fall, which is all that of ourselves we can do. "The just man," says the Apostle (Rom. i. 17), "liveth by faith :" this is the great and sure rule of the spiritual life. Do not guide yourself according to tastes, sensible experiences, or, on the other hand, by feelings of dryness and heaviness ; but walk by faith, which will show you that God ought to be equally served and adored in the time of tribulation as in that of consolation ; thus you will faithfully persevere in your spiritual exercises, without considering your repugnances or inclinations in the matter. Neither again will you be deceived if led by extraordinary ways, which are often the cause of much loss of time to directors, who have to discern whether the graces in question come from the Spirit of God, from the devil, or from the imagination, and frequently they are mistaken.

Those servants of God who concluded that St Teresa's extraordinary graces were illusions, because of sundry imperfections they noticed in her, were themselves deceived. "We draw a wrong inference," says the learned Bishop who has written the life of the Saint, "when we conclude that the gifts we perceive in a soul come not from the Spirit of God because that soul is imperfect, for they are sometimes bestowed in order to free it from its imperfections. If a soul, whatever interior words it may hear, or whatever vision it may behold, rests only on pure faith, leaving these things for what they may be worth, it will never swerve from truth : if they are the work of the devil, he will only reap shame and mortification thereby ; if of the Spirit of God, He will operate in the soul, independently of its attention or reflections." The practice of having pictures in our churches was introduced by the Spirit of God, and he who should blame this practice would be a heretic. Nevertheless, were we to stop short at the image, instead of passing on from the image to that which it represents, doubtless we should greatly err. Now, even the visions which the Spirit of God produces are but figures or images of the Divinity, they are not God Himself, and the Spirit of God accords them to us only in order to raise us to Him. Now, as faith is the closest means of union with God, we should abide by that. In fine, an entire and perfect abandonment to the Divine will with regard to all things and in all things, without any special desire, is the great secret for overcoming temptations. We must remember that we ought not to attach ourselves to the means which lead to God, however excellent they may be, nor to any practice, however good, but take it up and leave it according as it is fitting that we should do either one or the other, for all these means are not God, in whom alone we ought constantly to rest as our one only end.

Before concluding this subject, I am desirous to point out a common but dangerous temptation, which renders almost all our actions either profitless or imperfect : it is that the devil labours to make us be occupied with anything but what we are about. If you are engaged in prayer, he will make you think of some good action you have to perform : when you are performing this action, he will occupy your mind with some other ; and thus you are always thinking of something you are not doing, and never think well of your actual employment, or only give half your thoughts to it. Now, each moment has its own special blessing; do well whatever you are doing ; and that you may do it well, think of nothing else. The moment that is past is no longer yours ; the future is not yet come ; the present, therefore, is all you have. Here, then, is the devil's stratagem : by getting you not to attend to the present, and keeping you always rehearsing, as it were, for the future, he leaves you no moment really your own.

Another of his stratagems is to give you a taste for employments which are not suitable to your state. What good do you derive from letting your imagination run upon the life of a Carthusian, if your state is one of exterior occupations? And what is the use of Carthusians thinking of preaching or visiting hospitals, seeing that their call is to live the life of solitaries? We should do wonders, as we think, if we did those things which, however, we shall never do ; and we give no thought to performing well that which is our everyday duty. You are placed in a state where salvation is difficult, and in spite of yourself you must remain there. Lay it, then, seriously to heart that it is in this perilous state that you must work out your salvation, and do not waste your time in picturing to yourself other states of life on which you will never enter. Strive, however, in whatsoever condition you find yourself, to regulate your passions well; and know that the least is capable of plunging you into a miserable state of blindness, such as will even render you incapable of profiting by advice: and for this reason, that our passions, deceiving us, make us see things quite different from what they are. Thus, with a view to taking counsel, we describe them as we conceive of them, and counsel is given us according to our description, by which means we are often in great error, even while following advice, and this through our own fault, so that we are without excuse before God. Now, it is through our passions, which they make use of, that the devils deceive us in our view of things, as we have already remarked.

But the God of Heaven is more desirous of our salvation than hell is furiously bent on our destruction. As He thoroughly knows our powerlessness, in the excess of His divine mercies He gives us succour proportioned to our weakness; and while hell is perpetually on the watch to work our ruin, His eyes are ever lovingly intent upon defending us. He sends us the blessed angels of His heavenly court, by an order of Providence which the Church styles "wonderful," to uphold us in the battles which we must fight against these powers, whose force would infallibly overwhelm us without so special a protection. "A man's soul," says St Bernard, "is sometimes thrown into such great disorder, his mind is overcome with such distressing weariness, his heart is oppressed with such excruciating anguish, his body is so greviously afflicted, and the besetting temptation is so urgent, that without a powerful help he would succumb. At such a time," continues this Father, "it needs the assistance of the angels: it needs the consolation of these spirits of Heaven; in its present languid state it would be unable to walk; it is needful, then, that the angels should carry it in their arms. I hold as most certain that when the soul is in this condition, they support it, so to say, with both hands, bearing it so gently through all those perils which inspired it with most dread, that in some sort it feels them without perceiving them. We have to walk upon asps and basilisks ; we have to tread under foot lions and dragons; how necessary, then, is it that we should have the angels for our masters and guides! how needful it is that they should even carry us—us especially, who are like weak children ! But how easily do we traverse these dangerous roads when borne in their arms ! What do we fear? They are faithful, they are wise, they are powerful : let us but follow them, and never separate ourselves from them. Whenever, therefore, you are suffering from some great temptation or affliction, have recourse to your good angel ; say to him, ' My lord, save me, save me ! for I am on the point of being lost.'"

These are the sentiments of this great Saint, and they sufficiently manifest to us both the necessity and the sweetness of the protection afforded by these amiable princes of Paradise. As kings put robbers to death in their dominions to preserve the property and lives of their subjects, so do these glorious spirits destroy the power of the princes of hell, for the salvation of our souls and the glory of their Sovereign : thus it is said in Scripture (Tob. viii. 3; Apoc. vii. 1, xxii. 2) that they bind the devils ; that is to say, they restrain their power. The hermit Moses was greatly tormented by temptations of the flesh; and having sought the Abbot Isidore, to lay his troubles before him, and obtain some remedy, this abbot caused him to behold a troop of devils under sensible forms, prepared to attack him more fiercely than ever, the sight of which greatly afflicted this servant of God; but little by little he showed him a much more numerous band of holy angels armed for his defence, saying to him, "Know, my son, that with the Prophet Eliseus (4 Kings vi. 16) we must declare that we have more with us than against us ;" which so comforted him that he returned to his cell full of joy, and firmly resolved generously to resist all the assaults of the spirits of hell. I say the same thing to you, dear reader, after having spoken to you of the temptations of the devils, of their rage, of their power, of their stratagems, and of their multitude : we have more with us than against us. This truth is very sweet and well fitted to console us in all our troubles ; but I would beg you to meditate on it a little at your leisure.

We hope to return to the subject, with God's assistance, when treating of the confidence we ought to feel in the protection of the holy angels, of which we shall speak by and by. We will but add one word more. Know that a single devil, if God permitted it, would be able to destroy all the men on the face of the earth, were they all so many warriors armed *cap-à-pie ;* but know also that one single angel of Heaven is stronger, in the power he receives from God, than all the devils united. Remember, moreover, that all these blessed angels keep watch in our defence with a goodness beyond all imagination, and that the devils have a wonderful fear of them, even more than they have of the Saints, always excepting Her who can admit of no comparison, the incomparable Mother of God : for this reason, that the good angels having fought generously for the cause of God against these apostates at the time of their rebellion, they have merited to acquire a peculiar empire over them. Add to which, the remembrance which the devils have that they once enjoyed the same power of attaining to glory, whence they have so miserably fallen, as also the sight of the blessedness which these possess, and of which they are themselves deprived, strangely torments them.

Notes

[1] *E.g.* John x. 12 ; 1 Pet. v. 8 ; Ps. xc. 13.

[1] *E.g.,* Apoc. XX. 2 ; Ps. xc. 3; John viii. 44 1 John iv. 6.

[1] St Vincent de Paul.

[1] 2 Cor. xi. 14.

[1] St John of the Cross, canonised 1726.

[1] Phil. iv. 13.

NINTH MOTIVE.

The Great Assistance which the Holy Angels afford us at the hour of Death and after Death.

If one of the greatest philosophers held that death was the most terrible of all terrible things, ignorant as he was of that which follows, what ought Christians to think, to whom an all-gracious God has so mercifully revealed it? When the mind seriously considers that upon that tremendous moment hangs the decision of a blessed or miserable eternity, that few, very few, receive a favourable sentence, and that the greater number are condemned for ever to the unrelenting flames of hell, we must be more than insensible not to feel our heart pierced through and through with the extremest terror. But do we indeed believe those words of the Son of God, which teach us that the way of life is very narrow, and that few are they who find it? (Matt. vii. 14.) Do we believe that fearful truth which He has revealed to us, that very few are saved?[1] Do we reflect that we are ever advancing, or rather say, running towards death, where we must experience the truth of these infallible but terrible words, you who read this, and I who write it? What! is it indeed true that "the just shall scarcely be saved?" (2 Pet. iv. 18)—a thought which makes the most innocent souls tremble—and yet that the sinner may live in security, as if Paradise became his due at death, and that he had nothing to fear? O my God and my Lord! enter not into judgment with Thy poor servant, for in Thy Divine Presence no man shall be justified.[2] The holy Abbot Agathon, being at the point of death, was seized with extreme dread, and as his disciples, astonished, asked him if he had anything on his conscience which could give a reasonable cause for such apprehension, he replied, that, through the great mercy of our Lord, his conscience did not reproach him with anything, but that the judgments of God were very different from those of men. "All our justices," as Scripture teaches us (Isa. lxiv. 6), are but uncleanness when placed in the light of His divine purity.

If, therefore, the holy angels afford us great succour at that dreadful hour, then it is that they give us clear proof that they are our true friends. The true friend is known in affliction, and when we are in a great state of abandonment. Now, what affliction is like to death, when it is question of losing all or gaining all, when all leave us, and that without exception : husbands their wives ; fathers and mothers their children ; the most faithful friends those who are dearest to them? No one bears us company to the tomb ; the soul passes alone into Eternity; the body goes alone into the sepulchre. Oh, what an awful solitude ! and how fitting it is that it should often form the occupation of our thoughts ! All the creatures of earth abandon us ; not one amongst them comes to take our part at the judgment-seat of God ; the closest friendships of this world end at death. It is the privilege of angelic love, that it should extend beyond death itself : thus we cannot repeat too often, that in love the angels are incomparable.

Our Lord has revealed that those souls which had a particular devotion to the holy angels during their lifetime, receive extraordinary assistance from them at the hour of death ; and it is just that it should be so; for it is then that our Lord, the God of the great Eternity, rewards the worthy reception of His ambassadors; His honour is interested therein; for the good or bad treatment which the ambassadors of a king receive is referred to his person, and theologians hold that an affront offered to an ambassador is a legitimate ground for war. Now, the holy angels are the ambassadors of the King of kings ; what, then, do they not deserve who have scarcely noticed them, have scarcely thought of them, have scarcely thanked them, and have even treated them with the greatest ingratitude, with the utmost contempt, rejecting their counsels, and insolently disregarding their remonstrances? O my God, how many things will that moment of death reveal to us ! Blessed are those souls who, by their docility to the holy movements which these spirits of love have inspired, shall, by the love and devotion which they have shown to these charitable Intelligences, have prepared themselves to receive their special aid and the glorious reward of God !

After death, the holy angels present our souls before the tribunal of

God, and there defend our great eternal cause. Oh! well will it be for us to have at that time such good and zealous advocates. They accompany us into glory overflowing with joy. They visit us in Purgatory, and render us there all imaginable good offices which can be looked for from the most perfect and constant friendship. They console the suffering souls, but it is after their own angelic manner; that is to say, with consolations altogether heavenly, to which all the joys of this world are only shadows, and mere phantoms; they obtain their relief, or their deliverance, by the prayers, Masses, alms, and mortifications which they inspire persons to offer for them; and sometimes they even appear in visible shape, in order to urge them to do so, availing themselves of the species of our imagination to represent those who have been known to us, and this especially during sleep. In fine, the learned Suarez is of opinion, that at the day of judgment they will collect the ashes of those whose guardians they have been. Is it possible to conceive solicitude more loving or more faithful? But why all this precious love expended on such wretched creatures, if it were not that in the creature they regard God only?

Notes

[1] The statement in the text is not to be understood as if it were undoubtedly a revealed truth that very few are saved. Such a statement or doctrine is simply an *inference* which may or may not be deducible from our Lord's words. For, to the question, "Are they few that are saved?" He made no direct reply, but gave this practical exhortation, "Strive to enter by the narrow gate; for many, I say to you, shall seek to enter, and shall not be able" (Luke xiii. 23, 24). The reader will find the question debated by F. Rogacci, "Holy Confidence," chap. xxv.; and by F. Faber, "The Creator and the Creature," Book III. chap. ii., who also distinctly states the different opinions that have been held by theologians on the subject.

[2] Ps. cxlii. 2.

TENTH MOTIVE.

Devotion to the Holy Angels is a Mark of a High Predestination.

If our eyes were a little more open to eternal truths, our whole consolation would consist in the hope of being something hereafter in the glorious eternity. All that passes away is contemptible, and from the moment we know that a thing must have an end, whatever satisfaction it may afford us, whatever honour we may derive from it, we ought not to set much value on it. What has now become of those famous conquerors of the world, the Alexanders and the Cæsars? Where now are their laurels and their crowns? What remains to them of their triumphs and their victories? Come, my soul, let us visit in spirit those dungeons of fire and of flames where they have been burning for so many centuries, and let us learn in this dismal receptacle of all misery what the riches, the pleasures, and the honours of this perishable life have profited them. All these things have passed away, and they have passed away with all these things. Nothing now remains to them thereof save gloomy despair and ceaseless raving, torments which shall endure for ever, and which surpass all imagination. In truth, there is nothing that ought to affect us save that good and that evil which are eternal; and well may we here weep over the blindness of men.

The human heart is made for great things, and feels within it instinctive aspirations after greatness. Thus it is that men always covet something beyond what they possess. The common soldier would be a captain, the captain a general, the general would wish to be a prince, the prince would like to be a king, and a king would fain be the monarch of the whole earth, for it is a truth established by general induction applied to all classes of persons, that men always aspire to have something more than they possess, and to be something more than they are. It is only as respects Heaven and Eternity that their hearts are contented with such poor desires as are quite incredible. You will hear people say that they are perfectly satisfied to have the lowest place in Paradise. And, doubtless, even this would be a boon beyond our desert, who deserve only the lowest places in hell; but since our all-merciful God calls us to such exalted honours in a blessed Eternity, not to aspire generously after them implies the meanest spirit. "Be zealous for the better gifts:" so we are taught by the Holy Spirit (1 Cor. xii. 31). If you love honour, say the Saints, seek with courage that which shall endure for ever. St Teresa and St Francis Borgia protested that to acquire one single additional degree of glory, they would have been content to burn in the fires of Purgatory until the day of judgment. These enlightened souls knew well its value; they who are immersed in the flesh have not a glimpse of these things.

But, it will be asked, are not the blessed all perfectly satisfied? Assuredly they all are so, but their joy is not equal. Two men have each a vessel full of jewels : the vessels of both may be said to be quite full ; but if the vessel of the one can contain only a thousand precious stones, while the vessel of the other holds a million, their fulness is not equal, and the difference of their value is very great; in like manner all the blessed are fully satisfied, but the fulness of their satisfaction differs greatly. There is no comparison between the felicity of the Blessed Mother of God and that of the other saints. "As star differeth from star in glory, so also is the Resurrection of the dead" (1 Cor. xv. 41). The great St Teresa, of whom we have just spoken, says that in a supernatural vision she was shown the difference between the glory of an angel of one of the higher choirs and that of an angel of an inferior order, and that the difference surpasses all conception. The spiritual doctor Thaulerus, labouring to convey some idea of it, says that there is more difference between one of the blessed raised to the highest ranks of the empyrean and another who is not so exalted than there is between a king and a peasant. These magnificent elevations to which our holy vocation calls us, ought truly to animate our courage and to inspire us with generous longings for the honours of a glorious Eternity. But were there but this one only motive, that in our greater eternal glory God is more glorified eternally, surely a man must either renounce all claim to loving God, or he must exert himself to the death that he may become something in the Paradise of delights. A soul filled with the pure love of God would be willing to suffer ten thousand deaths, and endure ten thousand martyrdoms, if thereby it could add a single degree to His glory, and that degree were to last only a single moment. But here it is question, not of one degree only, but perhaps of a million and a hundred million degrees of glory, and that to last for an eternity ; and yet people do not stir. How true it is that we love God and His sacred interests but little ! How true it is that we love ourselves better than we love God !

Now devotion to the angels contributes marvellously to the perfection of divine love, and consequently to the increase of the glory of Heaven. These spirits are living flames of pure love; it is not possible to approach them often without taking fire and sharing their ardour. With the saints we become sanctified, with the angels we become all-angelic, that is to say, all-heavenly. It is the property of love to assimilate those persons who love each other. Now they cannot become like to us; their purity is incorruptible. It is necessary, then, that we should become like to them. Their life has always been a life of pure love, and thus our union with them will obtain us a certain relation therewith. Their solicitude in our behalf procures us great graces from God, and they never weary of seeking the augmentation of them, and of working in us, that, by the faithful use we make of them, our merits may increase every day more and more. They fashion us to perfection; they are the great masters of the spiritual life; they educate us therein with love ineffable. What proficiency should we not make under such direction, if we were better scholars ! When St Teresa was freed from her defects, and had entered on the pure ways of perfection, a heavenly voice said to her that she must no longer converse with men, but with angels. The conversation of creatures here below throws great obstacles in the way of holiness; that of the angels causes us to make admirable progress therein.

But as holiness is rare, devotion to these heavenly spirits is rare also; and among the small number of those who are devout to them, scarcely any are to be met with whose devotion extends beyond the angels of the lowest choir. There are very few who excel in devotion to the Seraphim, the Cherubim, and the other angels of superior hierarchies. We read, it is true, of a St Francis, of a St Elisabeth of Portugal, and of other holy persons who were admirably conspicuous for this devotion ; and so also they were great saints, and were established in the most perfect ways of holiness by the highest of the angelic bands ; as is seen in the person of the same St Francis, who received the sacred stigmata of our Lord through the ministration of a Seraph, and in that of St Teresa, whose heart was pierced with a wound of love by one of the most exalted Seraphim of Paradise. If we had a little pure love, it would be sufficient for us to know that, as God Only dwells in all the angels, so there is more of this God Only in those who are placed in the highest ranks. O God only, God only, God only !

ELEVENTH MOTIVE.
The Glory of the Most Holy Virgin.

For a heart which loves as it ought the most holy Mother of God, the promotion of her glory will be no weak motive. We read in the writings of persons of unimpeachable veracity, that there have been sinners, and very wicked sinners, who, in their deplorable state, were nevertheless so sensitive to it, that they protested that they would willingly sacrifice their lives to the honour of her who is the Queen of the blessings and delights of Paradise; and these desires have drawn down upon them such benedictions, that at last they have obtained, through the intercession of the Mother of Mercy, a Christian death, by a complete conversion and a notable change of life. If souls, then, living in rebellion against the laws of God, are capable of being touched with a regard for the honour of the august Queen of Heaven, how much more readily must pure and innocent souls, who, moreover, have a special devotion to her, be influenced by zeal for her sacred glory, a glory which she so justly deserves, and which we can never adequately render !

The angels, according to the testimony of St Bridget, from the very beginning of the world conceived so pure a zeal for the interests of this

Queen of Paradise, that they rejoiced more in her future birth than in their own creation. How many persons in the progress of time, after the pattern of these blessed spirits, and through their powerful aid, have preferred the interests of the Mother of God to their own, her honour to their honour, her being to their own being! I have known some who would have wished to possess a million of lives, that they might sacrifice them all to God for the glory of this incomparable Virgin; who would have been content to remain until the day of judgment in the midst of the dreadful flames of Purgatory, if it could in the least degree conduce to her honour ; who with all their heart would have been willing to be annihilated a million of times, if God thereby might be the more glorified. Truly a good heart never says, "It is enough," when it is question of the most pure Virgin—that is to say, within the limits of the order established by God. Ah ! we would wish to do everything, give up everything, and suffer everything for the love of her ; and after all, we well know that this would be but very little for her who has merited to be the Mother of God. These truths leave me no room to doubt but that the motive of her glory must be one of the most powerful that can be employed to promote love and devotion to the holy angels. Here, then, O ye souls who are devout to this glorious Virgin, I invite you to be devout also to the holy angels. Her glory is at stake : if you truly love her, this is to say all.

The Divine Mother is the general of the armies of God, and the angels form the glorious troops : thus they are the soldiers of her who alone is terrible as a whole army in battle array; and in the beginning they fought valiantly for her honour in opposition to Lucifer and the apostate angels, who would not submit themselves to her empire, God having revealed to them that she should one day be their sovereign. She is the august and triumphant Queen of Paradise; the angels are those faithful and generous subjects who honoured her, as we have just now said, before she was in being, and who glory in being subject to the laws of her kingdom. She is the Lady of Angels, and is often invoked under this title of Our Lady of Angels : they are, then, her servants, but such zealous servants that they await but the manifestation of her will to execute it, at its least sign, with a promptitude that is indescribable. She is even their friend: this is why in the Canticles (viii. 13) the Divine Spouse begs her to speak, and to make Him hear her voice, because, He says, "the friends are hearkening." Now these "friends" are the holy angels. We may say, moreover, that she is in some manner their Mother, and such is the opinion of many learned theologians. All these titles sufficiently show that the glory of this Queen, of this General, of this great and powerful Lady, is implicated in the consideration shown to her subjects, her soldiers, and her servants. The love which she bears them, treating them as her faithful friends, and even as her children, calls upon us for every possible reason to love what she loves, and to entertain the profoundest respect for those whom she desires to be honoured. Let us, then, praise and bless the holy angels, because the most pure Virgin, the august Queen and Lady of Angels, is praised and blessed by them; but, above all, let us praise and bless the Lord, who has made all that is great and worthy of praise, both in the Lady of Angels, and in the holy angels themselves; and that is God only, God only, God only.

TWELFTH MOTIVE.

God only.

When we have said God, we have said all, and nothing remains to be said, at least for pure love, whose whole pleasure it is to say it, and to say it alone. How should it say aught else, since it knows nothing else? "For us," said heretofore one of the greatest saints of this pure love, the divine Paul, "henceforth we know no man" (2 Cor. v. 16) ; for it is the property of this love to take away the perception of all that is not God, or, if it leaves the knowledge of anything else besides, it is only to behold it in its nothingness, in presence of this All-Adorable Being. Hence it is that he who is possessed with this pure love exclaims (Ps. lxxii. 25), "What have I in heaven or upon earth but Thee, O my God?" He has nothing on earth, he has nothing in heaven, because he has nothing but God only. Truly he thinks no more of pleasure, or reputation, or honour, or riches. He forgets natural goods, temporal goods, moral goods, spiritual goods, being filled only with the Sovereign Good. I will say more : he even loses the memory of himself; for he sees himself in his nothingness, like all other things ; in the affairs of his salvation, in his soul, in Heaven, in Eternity, he sees only the God of his soul, the God of Heaven, the God of Eternity. In vain shall you speak to him of anything else, his heart is ever turned towards God alone. His heart and his flesh are, as it were, in a holy trance as regards all created things : God only, the God of his heart and his eternal portion, is his one only all.

This is the state in which that Apostolic man was who declared (Gal. ii. 20) that he no longer lived, but that Jesus alone lived in him. The Holy Catherine of Genoa, whom one may call the Saint of the Divinity of Jesus Christ, could not even endure that word "me," that is to say, she could not in any manner regard her own interest. "O my God and my All !" said over and over again the humble St Francis ; and he spent nights and days in repeating these words of pure love. O sweet and savoury words ! as says the devout author of the "Imitation of Jesus Christ" (iii. 34), and it is a pleasure to repeat them ; for, indeed, it is most true, and a soul which loves purely will feel no doubt of its truth : Pure love in its perfection can see God only, rest in God only, say God only. It can rejoice, it can take pleasure in nothing save God only. It can care for nothing save His sacred interests. Its whole joy consists in being able to promote them, and all its sorrow springs from not having sufficiently regarded them. As for self-interest, it holds it in horror ; it is an abomination in its sight. No, we may truly say, it troubles itself no more about it than about the dust in the streets, and the care which it sees others bestowing upon themselves excites its deepest pity. The blessed possessor of this pure love has a holy contempt for his own interest; this is why it is to him a matter of indifference whether he be esteemed or despised by creatures—we may say more : the good are expelled from bis heart as well as others ; for there is no room there for any but God. Thus he does not concern himself if his reputation is ruined in the mind of good men, if he suffers contradiction from the servants of God, and if his best actions, performed under the inspiration of grace, meet with censure : so much less of creatures, he says to himself, so much more of God. The abandonment which he suffers constitutes his pleasure ; and in proportion to this abandonment his joy becomes greater, bis repose calmer, bis peace more profound; for bis highest and most exquisite joy is to come out from all that is created, in order to plunge into the Increate. Such were the dying sentiments of a holy soul in our day, which Father de Condren, an angelic man, admired, and which made him desire a like death. "I would wish," be said, "to die thus, uttering these words : I leave the created, to enter the Increate."

This Increate Being, who is God only, forms the whole occupation of a glorious eternity ; He fills alone all spirits and all the souls of the blessed who live therein ; and it would be most just that He should be the moving impulse of all hearts on earth, even as He is in heaven; but the greater number are attached to their own interests, and those who have loosened themselves from temporal interests still cling to self in their spiritual interests. A contemplative soul had one day a vision of the small number of the perfect lovers of the Son of God. It was manifested to him that out of a thousand, there were not a hundred who loved God; and out of these hundred, scarcely one who loved Him for His own sake. This sight cost him many tears. "Ah !" he exclaimed, "is it possible that there are so few hearts who love God after a perfect manner ; but amongst this small number of persons who love God for God, are any to be found who, loving God for God, love Him only, and love Him with fidelity?" The Blessed Henry Suso perceived scarcely any on his "last rock," that is to say, in the revelation which was made to him of the highest ways of perfection.* For this reason we have been compelled to suggest other motives in this little treatise, in order that men may at least love in some way or other; but these motives have none of them any value but because they terminate in God. It is God, it is God, who imparts their value to all things, and without Him all things are nothing.

The angelic nature is endowed with admirable perfections, but it derives them from God only, and it is only in Him that it possesses this glorious exaltation. "It is to God only," teaches the devout St Bernard, according to Scripture, "that honour and glory are due. It is true," says this holy Father, "that we must not be ungrateful to the holy angels ; we ought to have a great devotion for them, and be very thankful for all their goodness to us ; we ought to be full of love for creatures so noble, who love us so truly ; we ought to honour them to the utmost of our ability, and show them all manner of love and gratitude. Let us love and honour the angels," exclaims this holy man ; "nevertheless, to Him be all our love and all our honour paid from whom both we and they have received all we have wherewith either to love and honour, or to be loved and honoured ; and after all, what have we left to give, we who owe to God our whole heart, our whole soul, and all our powers?" It is, then, in God, and for God, that we must love the angels. God must be the great motive of all our devotions ; and blessed are those souls who act not only with a view to God, but with a view to God only ! It is for these souls who possess this holy disinterestedness that we have presented God only as a motive to the love and devotion which we invite them to practise towards these spirits of pure love. If it is God only whom they regard in all things, well and good : they have then every reason to love the angels, for they will find them wholly filled with God only.

The spouse, in the Canticles (iii. 1-4), seeks this God only amid the dark nights and obscurities of this life ; and in the fervour of the love which urges her, she runs in all directions ; she seeks her Beloved in the streets and public places ; she inquires for Him of all whom she meets, but all her efforts prove useless and ineffectual. At last she is met by the keepers of the city, and, after she has passed them a little way, she finds with joy the Beloved of her heart. Now this holy lover is the soul divinely smitten with pure love ; this is why she is a spouse, by reason of her union with God only. As her affections are not divided, she is worthy of the nuptial couch of the Divine Spouse; and so we find her saying (iii. 1,) that she sought Him in her bed. The Spouse tells her (iv. 9) that He has been wounded with love by one of her eyes, and one hair of her neck. He intends to mark thereby the unity of her affections ; He speaks of one hair only, because she has but one tie ; and of one of her eyes, because she looks at one thing only, and this it is that has ravished His Heart : she thinks of Him only, and desires Him only. She goes, then, about the streets and public places, seeking Him alone ; she cares not whether it be night ; she gives it not a thought that she walks in darkness, her love serves her as a torch and a guide. In like manner, the soul which is filled with pure love, leaning solely on faith, seeks God only unceasingly through all the veils of created things ; it seeks Him in the streets and public places, that is to say, everywhere. And as the spouse inquires for her Beloved, without even naming Him—the love with which she is transported making her believe that all the world knows the object of her affections—so also this soul cries everywhere, God Only ! without giving heed whether men understand this language or not ; she can afford to despise the blindness of those to whom such words are as an unknown tongue.

"The language of love," says St Bernard, "is a barbarous tongue to those who love not." "If I speak," says that holy lover, St Augustine, "to a person who loves, he well understands what I say. If I speak to a frigid heart, devoid of love, it understands me not." The spouse finds not her Beloved, because her Beloved is God only; and in all men there is something else besides God only—excepting always Her with whom comparison is inadmissible, the ever-incomparable Virgin, Mother of God. Sin is to be found in all, either mortal or venial, or at least original, if it be true that some Saints have been preserved from venial sin, as is the opinion of some with respect to St John the Baptist. But at last the Beloved is found after meeting those who keep watch over the city; for these guards who are stationed on the walls of Jerusalem, and who keep continual watch, are the holy angels; and on meeting them the Beloved is found, because there is not, and never was, in them aught save God only. It is true that the spouse declares that she found her Beloved after she had passed these guards a little way, because pure love does not stop short either at the beauty or at any of the other perfections of the angels, however lovely and lovable they may be; it passes by all these, and goes straight to God only, the Author of all these graces and all these gifts, the Beginning and the End of all things. He who possesses pure love is in a state of universal death to everything; and it is this death which teaches the science of pure love. This is why St Bernard desired to die the death of the angels, meaning by this death a perfect detachment from every created thing; and, in the desire of this pure love, he ardently longed for this holy destitution of all that is not God. "Where is wisdom to be found?" says holy Job (xxviii. 12-22) ; it is not to be "found in the land of them that live in delights. The depth saith, It is not in me: and the sea saith, It is not with me. Whence, then, cometh wisdom? It is hid from the eyes of all living"—of all those who live in themselves, and it is even unknown to "the fowls of the air," that is, to the most exalted minds, the doctors, the learned, in fine, to all these great men. "Destruction and death" alone have said that they have learned something of it, and "have heard of the fame thereof." "O My Father !" said our Divine Master (Matt. xi. 25), "I give thanks to Thee, because Thou hast hid these things from the wise and prudent, and hast revealed them to little ones." O blessed, then, are the poor in spirit! O blessed are the dead who die in the Lord, to whom is given the knowledge of God only, and whose will is united to God only !

Such souls, seeing only this Infinite Majesty in the holy angels, are ravished at the blessed revelation they behold of It in these glorious bands. "O heavenly armies !" they exclaim, "how lovely are you in your beauty, seeing that you are but pure and spotless mirrors of the beauty of God ! We are constrained to love you, for nothing save God is to be seen in you ; you have ever been filled with Him ; and, never having belonged to yourselves, you have been possessed by Him alone. Great princes of the empyrean, how can we help loving you, since you have ever loved and have ever been loved by Him who is Love ; since you have ever loved as much as it was in your power to love? for it is most assuredly true that never for one single moment have you been without love, without pure love. O my soul ! if our inclinations ought to be ruled by those of a God, the angels ought indeed to be the worthiest objects of our tenderest affections. O ye desires of my heart ! go, then, nay run, fly to these enrapturing beings, these amiable spirits, these glorious princes of a blessed Eternity. God only, God only, God only!"

Note

* See Note D.

PART II.

PRACTICE OF THIS DEVOTION.

FIRST PRACTICE.
To have a Particular Devotion to the Angels, Archangels, and Principalities.

The three orders of the third and last hierarchy of angels are composed of the Angels, the Archangels, and the Principalities, or, according to some, the Virtues. This last hierarchy is specially engaged in the care of men, of kingdoms and provinces, and of other things, which peculiarly regard the good of men. Our Guardian Angels are generally taken from the third order of this hierarchy; the Archangels watch over empires and provinces; and the Principalities communicate to the Angels and Archangels the orders of Divine Providence which they receive from the second hierarchy. They are called Principalities, according to St Gregory, because they are the princes of the heavenly spirits of the two inferior orders of their hierarchy. The Angels manifest the Divine will in ordinary matters ; the Archangels make it known in such as are of greater moment ; and both are informed and enlightened therein by the Principalities, who represent in a special manner the empire and sovereignty of God. Now the loving charity of the blessed spirits of this hierarchy towards men is so exceedingly great and so admirable, that we shall never be able to make any adequate return either of gratitude or of homage ; but at least let us love them as much as is in our power. I well know that this love will never equal their merits ; God grant that it may be to the utmost of our ability, according to what God requires of us, and in such a manner as is pleasing to Him.

Let us, then, have a singular devotion to our good Angel Guardians : and indeed it is difficult not to have it, and we must be utterly blind and heartless not to entertain towards them all those sentiments of perfect gratitude which we are capable of feeling. Let us honour much the Guardian Angels of the heathen, and let us from time to time go in spirit to converse with them and bear them company, to express the regret of our hearts at the unbelief of those of whom they have the charge. Alas ! so far from thanking them for their loving care, these poor infidels do not even know that they are assisted by them. Admire these princes of heaven, and their unwearied patience ; consider how many millions of them there are in barbarous lands, who keep untiring watch over these unhappy beings, without ever experiencing from them the least token of gratitude ; endeavour to compensate, according to your poor ability, for their neglect; let their ingratitude or their ignorance touch your heart with feelings of love towards these spirits of love. Communicate from time to time in honour of them ; practise mortifications, give alms, hear Mass, and have Masses offered for the same object ; above all, as we have said, in spirit bear them company, and go often to visit them. Ah ! if the princes of the earth; the kings of this world, were in some place where you could enjoy the honour of saluting them, conversing with them at your ease, gaining their friendship, and thus insuring their favour, how would you act? Now here are princes and kings of the empyrean, whom you may salute whenever you please, whose good graces you may gain, and who will be certain to recompense, sooner or later, the affection which you have shown them. As they are so utterly neglected, they will have the greater reason to love you all the more. A great and generous king who, when banished from his kingdom, and deserted by his subjects, should receive some important services, would not fail to requite them conspicuously when he was peaceably restored to his dominions ; judge hence what you may expect from these noble spirits. Perform devotions in their honour, to obtain from the Divine Goodness the conversion of the nations under their care, in order that, learning to know the Adorable Jesus, and Mary His sweet Mother, they may also know and honour these nobles of the court of Heaven. I say the same with respect to the Guardian Angels of heretics, and of all those poor country people who have scarcely any more knowledge of the holy angels than have those who live in the midst of heathen lands. Adopt the same practices with reference to these, and pray often that, being known and loved, they may also be duly honoured.

Be devout to the Guardian Angels of your friends ; they render you in many instances greater services than you are aware; and sometimes they even give you assistance which you do not receive from your own Angel Guardian. There are occasions on which they interest themselves in your behalf for the sake of those of whom they have the care, knowing that your friendship is profitable to them for the good of their souls. As there is nothing of which these holy spirits have a greater horror than of bad or dangerous friendships, so also one of the things which affords them most consolation is a holy union in the interests of God. The devils do all they can to make men contract evil friendships, and the good angels to break them. The holy angels labour to unite those who are seeking God, and the devils neglect nothing to part them, and to create disunion between them. A holy person having contracted a truly Christian friendship with another, the devil, envious of the good which it was producing, seized one of them, and threw him down some steps to the ground. The Guardian Angel of the friend came speedily to his help, and preserved him from injury; but what is remarkable is this, that it was the friend's Angel-Guardian, and not the Guardian of him who was cast down by the devil.

In the number of your friends, spiritual directors ought to hold a very prominent place; beseech their good angels to inspire them with such counsels as are purely conformable to the Divine will. You should also highly honour those of your father and mother, of your relations, and of other persons with whom you are connected, and who render you, or may render you, some service. The honour which you pay to their angels will not be without fruit, and you will obtain through their means what you would never gain in any other way. Remember, also, the Angel-Guardians of all those persons who are kind, or have been kind to you; these angels have more to say than you think to the benefits you have received from them. Honour the angels of your enemies, of those who are opposed to you in any way whatever: this is the true means to soften their hearts; or, if it be more for the glory of God that you should suffer at their hands, these glorious spirits will obtain you special graces to make a good use of your sufferings, and cordially to love those who hate you or cause you trouble. Do not forget to pay your homage to those princes of Heaven who guard the Sovereign Pontiff, the Bishops, and other persons who preside over the Church, as well as kings, princes, governors, and other administrators of temporal things.

The Archangels of kingdoms and of provinces must also be objects of your devotion, as also those of the towns and villages in which you dwell and through which you pass. This was a devotion practised by that holy man, Father Peter Faber, first companion of St Ignatius, and St Francis de Sales makes honourable mention of it in his "Introduction to a Devout Life." St Francis Xavier, when going to the Indies, paid his devotions to the holy Archangel of those countries, and while he was still at Rome he was visited, and powerfully urged to pass over to these foreign lands, by an angel in the garb of an Indian. That Macedonian who appeared to St Paul (Acts xviii. 9), and pressed him to go into Macedonia to preach the gospel there, was doubtless the Archangel of that country.

We have already observed that there are angels who have the care of the heavens, of the sun, of fire, of air, of the waters, of the earth, and even of the other creatures in the world; and the Angelic

Doctor is of opinion that God employs the ministry of these heavenly spirits in all that He ordinarily works here below. It is through their instrumentality that the scourges of His divine justice are averted; that fires and conflagrations are extinguished; that inundations subside; that pestilence is abated; that the air is purified; that lands become fertile; in fine, that we receive all sorts of good things, and are preserved from a multitude of evils, and all this often without our perceiving it, without our knowing the obligations we are under to the holy angels. Let us, then, to-day form a good resolution to thank them sometimes for these services, and to invoke them, and cause them to be invoked, by public and private prayers, in time of famine, war, or pestilence, as well as in other sicknesses and necessities; for fair weather, and for rain, for the fruits of the earth, and in all our various needs. We have also said that they are the protectors to whom we must have recourse in all things, and the most mighty whom Heaven has given us to destroy all the power of our adversaries.

Our churches, and even altars, have angels who guard them; and they gather in troops around the tabernacles where reposes the Blessed Sacrament of the Altar, to pay their court to their Sovereign. Many Saints have beheld them paying their adoration to their great King and ours. A holy hermit was told by an angel himself that he had the guardianship of an altar, and that he had never left it since its consecration. It is to these angels we ought often to have recourse, that they may supply for our negligences, our tepidity, and our want of respect in presence of a God of Infinite Majesty in the Most Blessed Sacrament; that they may appease His anger, justly irritated by so many irreverences committed in our churches, and that they may open the eyes of Christians, and those the greater number, who give such little heed to the veneration due to our temples. It is good to associate ourselves with these heavenly spirits, uniting our reverence and love with theirs, and, after the example of the Psalmist (cxxxvii. 1), sing the praises of God in their sight.

And here, O my Lord and my God, suffer me to sigh and pour forth my heart before Thy Divine Majesty, because of the deplorable blindness of Thy people, who are the people of light. Is it, then, Thou,

O God, Infinitely Adorable, who art hidden with all Thy perfections under the veil of the Eucharistic species? Is it Thy Body, Thy Blood, Thy Soul, Thy Divinity which is really and truly present in the Blessed Sacrament of the Altar? Is it possible that men still retain any faith in these most indubitable truths? Or is it an illusion—this that is so visible and palpable to us every day in the treatment Thou receivest in this august mystery? Our hair stands on end, and our whole body trembles with dread, when we consider the abominable profanations of this Sacrament of love committed by sorcerers,* and the impieties practised by heretics towards this adorable mystery. But who could have conceived the irreverence of the faithful, of those who believe and who fear, and who declare themselves ready to die for this truth, that Thou, O my God, O Adorable Jesus! art most truly present in the Divine Eucharist? Ye angels of Heaven, what a spectacle does such blindness present to you! Ah! we may well say that your patience takes its rule from that of the meek Saviour, for yon to be able to endure such irreverences. No; we must declare it before the face of Heaven and earth: we cannot recover from our astonishment, we are lost in amazement, when we consider darkness so appalling. O my God, O my God! are we living in a Catholic country? Are our churches and altars in the possession of the faithful? Have these people, whom we see trooping in crowds to them, any vestige of faith? Is there anything to give us pleasure in what we there witness? And if there be any truth in all we believe, can we live, can we possibly continue, in a place where our Master is so unworthily treated?

Listen, O Christians! and listen attentively. It is an indubitable truth that in the minutest particle of the Most Holy Sacrament the great God of everlasting ages is really present. All Catholics confess this. But what care is taken to prevent the profanations which hence may occur? Oh! how many priests are there, little instructed in the holy rubrics, or little intent on the care of the Adorable Body of a God, who give scarcely any heed diligently to collect the particles which may remain on the paten, or on the corporal! The generality of portable altars are so small that the sacred chalice cannot be moved a little on one side or backward, in order to allow the paten to be placed further on the corporal, and the corporal itself to be raised, so that the particles which adhere to it may fall easily on the paten; hence it frequently happens that the Body of the Son of God remains there, and falls to the ground, or is carried away with the corporals when they are taken to be washed. How often may one see corporals so ragged or so dirty as to send a revulsion to the heart ! Experience shows that in religious houses, where a paten is used at the grate in time of communion, or some red or green taffety—because upon linen the particles of the Sacred Host, being also white, would be undiscernible—experience, I say, shows that often many particles are imperceptibly detached from the Blessed Sacrament ; consequently, in places where there is only an ordinary linen cloth, they either fall on the cloth or on the ground, unless the priest takes extreme care to carry the ciborium in such a manner as that it shall always be underneath the Sacred Host, which is often almost impossible. If they fall on the cloth they also fall to the ground ; for at each fresh communion the cloth is dropped, and no further attention is given to it ; it is afterwards folded up without being examined, and were it otherwise, these little particles, which are well-nigh imperceptible, could not be discovered on account of the linen being white. Here, then, is the Body of a God trodden underfoot and sometimes under the shoes of a vile creature !

How many tabernacles are there in which spiders and dust are allowed to harbour, and which are so imperfectly closed that people would not endure to have in their houses wardrobes containing the most trifling things so insecure and so dirty ! How many priests leave the tabernacle key in the church, instead of locking it up by another key, and carrying that key away, which they ought to do, if they do not take away the key of the tabernacle itself ! And how many profanations result from this want of care ! We speak advisedly. How often are miserable rags shamelessly employed to cover ciboriums in which are contained the Divinity, the Soul, the Body, and the Blood of the Adorable Jesus ! And yet Christians know and see these things, and scarcely any one thinks of providing a remedy. You hear people say—O my God ! how often have I heard it ! how often has it been said to me—"We have no money to buy a little linen to make corporals and purificatories;" the poorest peasants will contrive to have enough for their shirts and collars ; but as for Thee, my God, Thou hast not credit enough to raise as much!*

Oh ! ye gentlemen and ladies, who have so much fine linen, so much handsome furniture, so much silver plate, and that sometimes even for the meanest uses, what will you say at the day of judgment? Ye pastors, who are entrusted with the care of this Adorable Body, what will you answer Him ? Will it be a sufficient excuse for you to allege on that dreadful day that the Church was too poor to provide corporals, or to pay for a decent ciborium or chalice ? The retrenchment of a banquet, of a few dinners, or of some other expense, would more than suffice—I mean, for ciborium and chalice, for as to the corporals, two crowns or less would be enough, and indeed they are sometimes so narrow that the priest, after consecration, can scarcely keep his hands on them. You will see a pewter chalice in a gentleman's private chapel ; and in the chapels of not a few ecclesiastics who are in the receipt of good revenues, we see the same thing, and a very scanty supply of linen and ornaments for the sacred altar. But is it possible that what we are saying is true ? Is there any faith in the Most Holy Sacrament still surviving among Christians ? Is the thought not enough to rend the heart in twain with grief ? Who will give me a voice of thunder, that I may call aloud to the children of men throughout the whole earth, and reproach them with their hardness and deadness of heart?

O angels of Paradise ! I turn to you, knowing well the insensibility of men : do you take charge—I conjure you, I entreat this favour of you, prostrate at your feet, in the bitterness of my heart, and bathed in tears—do you take charge of the Body of our Sovereign. Watch over every particle of the Sacred Host ; inspire priests with a holy solicitude to preserve them in perfect cleanliness before consecrating them, and to use every possible means to prevent the profanation of those that are reserved after consecration. Stimulate all prelates, archdeacons, and other visitors of churches, to give most diligent heed that the Body of a God may be both treated and preserved with all possible respect. Enlighten more and more the minds of those who have the training of ecclesiastics in the seminaries, that they may give the necessary instructions in a matter of such high importance. Order it so that the subject may be introduced and discussed in clerical conferences, and counsel taken concerning the needful remedies to be applied. Touch the hearts of such as are possessed of the means, that in the different dioceses associations may be formed for collecting funds to provide ciboriums, chalices, and corporals. I know from my own personal experience, derived from the great number of visitations which my office obliges me to make in the course of the year, that with a little zeal it would be easy in a few years, through the exertions of the bishop, the archdeacons, the parish priests, the nobility, and a few other persons in easy circumstances, to provide decent tabernacles, ciboriums of silver, or, in places liable to be robbed, ciboriums of copper, into the interior of which a sort of silver cup might easily be fitted with perfect exactness, wherein to deposit the Sacred Hosts : the cost would be small, two crowns or thereabouts sufficing. This sort of ciborium is quite as suitable as the little silver boxes commonly employed, and is better adapted for use, because it holds a larger number of Hosts, which are not exposed, as in the little boxes, to sundry risks which occur when they are used for giving communion at Easter and other solemn festivals, at which times a great concourse of persons approach the Holy Table; it would be easy, I say, to have decent tabernacles as well as ciboriums, to make use of none but silver chalices, and to furnish every church and chapel with proper corporals and purificatories.

Sublime intelligences, loving guardians of chapels, make known the miserable state in which they are left ; cause them to be carefully visited, for very often they are quite neglected, and it is the parish church alone which is visited ; the consequence of which is, that the very names of the incumbents are scarcely known, who frequently never set foot in them, eat up the revenues with impunity, disregard the charges attached to them, or acquit themselves only of a part of them, and expend nothing on the maintenance of these chapels or priories, but leave them in a lamentable condition, without ornaments, without furniture, so that they look rather like barns or stables than sanctuaries appropriated to the consecration of the Body and Blood of a God.

Oh! what a reckoning shall prelates have to give of these places, where the most august of our sacred mysteries is treated with such habitual irreverence through their want of care: and here I must not omit to mention a circumstance which I have observed during my visitations. If a church lacks a banner or a pall, great eagerness is shown to obtain the money to provide one; if the subject be mentioned, everybody listens, and is ready to lend his aid; all exclaim against the disgrace; and although the expense may be pretty considerable, means are found to meet it. But let a couple of crowns be wanted to put a ciborium in decent order, after the manner described above, or to purchase corporals, every one is silent, no one cares to listen. Such is the utter blindness of Christians, proof sufficient of the hardness of hearts and the want of faith Sometimes people will object to having a ciborium or chalice of silver; they will insist that a pewter one will answer the purpose very well, that it has been hitherto deemed sufficient; and a wish will be expressed to convert the church plate into money. I earnestly commend the matter to pious souls, that they may devise some means of remedying such a deplorable state of things; and I conjure with tears all whose hearts are touched with zeal for the glory of the Adorable Jesus in the Most Blessed Sacrament, to practise frequent devotions in honour of the holy angels, and especially of those who abide in our churches, who encompass the Most Holy Sacrament, and who keep watch over altars, that they may ask pardon of the Divine Majesty for our irreverence, our coldness, our blindness, our insensibility; and that they may inspire us with the knowledge of the suitable means to obtain for this Mystery of Love the respect which is Its due.

What Father de Bary, a Jesuit, relates in his excellent book on "Devotion to the Angels," plainly proves that Communities and Confraternities have their angels also who watch over them. He affirms that he was informed by the confessor of a young man of the town of Eu, who lay dangerously ill, that towards the hour of noon, on a certain Wednesday, two angels, all-resplendent with majesty and beauty, appeared to him, and consoled him to the very moment of his death, which occurred on the following Saturday, as they had predicted to him. Now one of these angels told him that he was his angel-guardian, and the other the tutelary angel of the

Confraternity of the Blessed Virgin established in that city, in the College of the Company of Jesus. The angel of the Confraternity, moreover, said to him that they were sent by the command of the most holy Mother of God thus to assist him, on account of the patience with which he had borne some ill-treatment which he had suffered from his father and mother, especially as he might have avoided it if he had so willed, and also because he had faithfully observed the rules of the Confraternity.

It is a holy practice to implore the aid of the angels of the diocese in which we reside, and of the guardian angels of its bishop and of those under him, that they may succeed in establishing the reign of Jesus Christ in the hearts of the faithful who dwell there, that they may destroy the empire of Satan, and receive the lights and strength necessary to maintain holy discipline in the diocese; and that they may defeat the malice and wiles of the devils, who are ever labouring to counteract the means which God is pleased to employ for the promotion of His divine interests.

Finally, we must be devout to the Angels, to obtain through them purity of mind and body, charity towards our neighbour, and also patience; to the Archangels, to obtain through them a zeal for the interests of God, both for ourselves and others, especially for those who govern in Church and State, for all who are vested with authority, and for the spiritual and temporal good of kingdoms and provinces ; to the Principalities for the reformation of our own interior. Man is a little world in himself, and he is bound to govern his passions, and rule as a sovereign over them. But since his power is marvellously weakened by sin, he needs support, that he may not let himself be overcome by himself. The Principalities, who bear this glorious title on account of the rule which God has given them over the inferior angels, will render him powerful assistance if he strives to make himself not unworthy of it ; but to this end he must honour with profound reverence these great princes of Paradise.

Notes

* See Note E.
* See Note F.

SECOND PRACTICE.

To Honour especially the Powers, the Virtues, and the Dominations.

The second hierarchy is composed of the Powers, the Virtues, and the Dominations, or, according to some who place the Virtues in the last hierarchy, the Principalities, the Powers, and the Dominations. The Dominations, as lords or primates of the second hierarchy, give orders in the things of God; the Virtues impart strength to obey them; and the Powers resist the devils who oppose their execution, overthrowing their might, and removing all the obstacles that stand in the way.

It is, then, the Dominations who communicate the commands of God, and make known to us His holy will. Oh, happy we, if we could well discriminate between the Divine will and our own ! How often does the love of ourselves and of creatures, the invariable effect of which is to darken the mind, deceive us, and cause us to mistake our will for that of God ! A soul which is but even slightly touched with Divine love would with difficulty bring itself to oppose the will of God when it fully recognises it ; but our corrupt nature insensibly glides in, and easily persuades us that what we wish is what God wills. We would wish the will of God to be done, but we should be well pleased that our own should be done also ; and so we endeavour to reconcile the Divine will with our own will This disorder is much greater among spiritual persons than is commonly supposed. Now devotion to the Dominations is a great remedy thereto, since it is the special office of these spirits of light to make known to us the commands of God ; they are, so to say, the secretaries of state of the great King Jesus.

But it is not sufficient to know the commands of God, we must proceed to execute them. He who knows the will of his master, and performs it not, shall be severely punished. O my God ! how meet it is that Thy creatures should be perfectly subject to Thee ! O Lord, who is like unto Thee ! Who can appear in Thy Divine Presence and be worthy of regard ? The whole universe before Thee is but as a drop of dew, and all the nations are as nothingness. What a wretched thing it is not to fly at the least intimation of Thy good pleasure ! Oh, the good pleasure of God ! May it he for all eternity our only pleasure ! Come, my soul, let our movements be ever in that direction ; let the world, and everything in the world, be always an abomination to thee. O my God! may Thy will be done, as in Heaven, so on earth ! Nevertheless, with all our good purposes we accomplish nothing of any worth; our eye reaches farther than our arm. From the summit of a tower we can survey a very difficult road we have to traverse, and the view of it is unquestionably easy in comparison with the toil to be endured in actually proceeding along it : so it is with our reasonings; it seems to us as if nothing would stop us; and when the hour of combat arrives, they who in imagination have discomfited giants and monsters, are disheartened at the sight of pigmies. We are naught but sheer weakness ; we are ruled by our senses, by our inclinations. You will see devout persons, who seem to be working wonders, lay down their arms to some slight inclination, and allow themselves to be overcome by the merest nothing : it is a most pitiable spectacle; and yet, after all, we are not really aware of our own utter powerlessness; we are much more feeble than our imaginations can ever conceive. Let devotion to the Virtues, then, be our resource, that we may be sustained by these mighty Intelligences; let us invoke them in our weaknesses ; let us recommend this devotion to those who so constantly fall, notwithstanding all their good desires; let us call them to our aid; let us love them and bless them when we have overcome some attachment, or resisted some natural inclination. St Gregory is of opinion that it is through the instrumentality of the Virtues that God ordinarily performs most of His miracles. Have a special love, then, for these angels ; and in extraordinary necessities of mind or body, in times of epidemics and other public afflictions, have recourse to them. It is by them also that God governs the seasons, the visible heavens, and the elements generally, although angels of the lowest hierarchy have the special charge of them. In times of plague, inundations, and other such like evils, one of the best things we can do is to invoke and honour them.

We have elsewhere detailed the different temptations of the devils, their stratagems, their malice, and their might, and we said that of ourselves we are unable to resist these invisible powers; we also said that the holy angels have been given to us to enable us to triumph over them. But here we must remark, that it is to the particular choir of the Powers that God has given a special strength to bring to naught all the efforts of these malicious spirits; and one of the greatest secrets of the spiritual life is to apply ourselves assiduously to honour the blessed spirits of this choir. It is not within the limits of my capacity nor of that of any other man to exalt sufficiently the marvellous effects which result therefrom. According to the little light I possess, this devotion to the Powers ought to be encouraged as one of the most necessary and most profitable. When we see storms gathering either in the Church or in the State, combinations to resist those who are working for the glory of God, extraordinary conspiracies to defeat some great good which is being planned in dioceses, towns, country districts, and provinces— then it is that we ought to perform frequent devotions in honour of these Powers of Heaven, that they may overturn and destroy all the might and miserable plottings of hell.

THIRD PRACTICE.
To have a Profound Reverence and Extraordinary Love for the Thrones, Cherubim, and Seraphim.

The first hierarchy is composed of the Seraphim, Cherubim, and Thrones; it receives its lights immediately from God, which by it are communicated to the two other hierarchies.

The Seraphim excel in the pure love of God only, their very name signifying ardour and burning. All the angels are admirable in the love of God, but the Seraphim are incomparable therein. All these angelic spirits love exceedingly, but when we speak of the love of the Seraphim, we mean a fervour of love which is beyond compare—always excepting the most holy Virgin, the Queen of holy love. Seraphic love signifies intense love, which is ever burning and consuming. The great St Denis mentions eight properties which belong to it, and which he compares to those of fire. Fire is in constant motion, and the spirits of the Seraphim are continually tending in an ineffable manner towards God. Fire is ever active, and the Seraphim are incessantly intent on God only, never being occupied, even for the space of the briefest moment, either with themselves or with any created thing. Fire is inflexible, and the love of the Seraphim is invincible; nothing can prevail against it. Fire is intensely hot; and the love of the Seraphim is a burning love. Fire, so long as it flames, never loses its light, and the strength of Seraphic love abides ever in its fulness. Fire is penetrating; and the love of the Seraphim, not satisfied with an ordinary degree of union with God, desires the closest and most intimate. Fire not only penetrates what is combustible, but permeates it throughout; and Seraphic love plunges, loses, and ingulfs itself in the abyss of the Divinity by a glorious transformation. Fire communicates warmth and purifies; the Seraphim carry love and light into all the choirs of the inferior angels.

Light is attributed specially to the Cherubim, as love to the Seraphim. They are not only styled learned in the divine science of Heaven, but St Gregory affirms that they have the very fulness of it. Divine light imparts to them admirable knowledge, and the holy effulgence with which they are replenished is reflected in abundant streams upon the other hierarchies. They are represented by the Prophet Ezekiel (i. 18) under a sensible figure, with eyes on all sides, because these spirits are all light and brilliancy.

The Thrones are thus styled with a reference to the thrones of the sovereigns of the earth, because as these material thrones are raised above the ground, so also these celestial Thrones are exalted to a most sublime height, into a close vicinity to the glory of the Majesty of God; with this difference, that the great ones of the earth are seated, support themselves, and repose upon their thrones, whereas, on the contrary, the Thrones of Heaven derive their firmness and all their repose from the Sovereign of Paradise. We are told, it is true, as St

Bernard remarks, that God is seated upon these spirits of peace, whence also they are styled Thrones; but God (continues this Father) would not be seated upon them if they did not repose upon Him : hence flows that incomprehensible peace which they possess, surpassing all that we can possibly conceive. We must add, that, like as kings sometimes cause themselves to be borne in their royal chair, so also God in a certain manner conveys His Spirit by these angels, and communicates It to the inferior angels and to men; as kings give judgment upon their thrones, so also it is from the midst of these Thrones that God pronounces His decrees: it is there that the Dominations learn them ; it is there that His Divine judgments and counsels are manifested.

If this be so, we may well say that we are in every way bound to love the Thrones, the Cherubim, and the Seraphim ; and, if it be most meet that we should feel respect and love for all the angels, for these we must entertain unparalleled reverence and surpassing love. The Lord, says the Scripture (Ps. lxxv. 3), has chosen His abode in peace. In time of war, then, let your devotions be offered to the Thrones, to obtain that peace which the world cannot give. Beseech of them that you may enjoy it with yourself, with God, and with your neighbour. "If I did yet please men," said the great Apostle (Gal. i. 10), "I should not be the servant of Jesus Christ." There are certain persons, preachers, superiors, men who hold offices in the Church, who have so great a dread of displeasing creatures, and so great a desire to content them, who fear so much the censure of the world and the judgment which may be passed upon them, who are so alarmed at contradiction, that they allow those who are under them to wage war against God by sin and infidelity to their trusts. This is the peace which the Son of God protests aloud (Matt. x. 34) that He came not to bring upon earth ; and thus our amiable Lord was ever on earth a sign of contradiction (Luke ii. 84) ; men would not endure His presence among them, and it cost Him at last His Divine Life.

In order to be firmly established in this divine peace which all devils and men united cannot disturb, we must (to express it in a few words) fear nothing and hope nothing from any living creature. In these few words is comprehended a peace which is beyond all thought. To this we may add, Believe only in God, hope only in God, love but God only ; never believe the world, or its arguments, or its maxims ; never hope for anything from the world, from its honours, its pleasures, or its goods ; never love the world, and behold you are settled in a profound peace. No longer make account of any created things ; never look at them save in their nothingness ; never desire any share in the esteem or in the heart of any one ; banish the good from your heart as well as others ; make no exception ; be ready to suffer at the hands of all creatures without reserve, of your nearest friends as well as of your enemies; never believe that any injury can be done to you, but live in a state of entire abandonment to Divine Providence, prepared to enter upon ways the most distressing, be they exterior or interior ; make no reservation with respect to any particular cross ; entertain no longer any desires ; lose them all in the good pleasure of God ; let God alone suffice you, and behold you already enjoy the peace of Paradise ! And here you must remember that disturbance in the inferior part is quite compatible with the peace which resides in the depths of the soul, and which sometimes even remains hidden from us ; thus it frequently happens that we are never in a better state than when we think ourselves in the worst The devil gives us a false peace, which sooner or later fails to keep out disquietude and trouble. However, if peace is the gift of gifts, and if our Lord ordains it through the ministry of the blessed Thrones, no doubt can remain but that we ought to have a very singular devotion to these spirits of peace.

I say the same with respect to the Cherubim, since they are the angels of the most brilliant lights of Paradise, who best know how to instruct us in the excellent science of the Saints. It is said with truth, that we already know more than we perform ; that in the ways of virtue light abounds more than practice ; nevertheless, it is also true, though you will scarcely believe it, that perfect light is rare. I speak not here of that light of human science which learned men derive only from their books—we all know that such light is common enough in our day—but of that of the Saints, which is more often to be found in some poor lay brother, or some poor simple woman (*simple femmelette*) of truly mortified life, than among the learned. Oh, how rare it is, not only to love contempt, abjection, poverty, self-renunciation, the hidden and unknown life, but even to be thoroughly persuaded of the excellence of these things! It is true you will hear people occasionally talking about them because they have been reading of them, or have heard the subject treated in a conference, but this does not spring from any thorough conviction of the mind; or, if the soul is touched with these truths, it is but very superficially. It is at the feet of Jesus Christ Crucified that this science is learned ; and this, not so much by means of the exercise of the understanding in prayer, by the discursive method, or by meditation, as by a bright supernatural light which is vouchsafed, and which is scarcely ever given save to the poor, the abject, and the humble. Few, even among those who make profession of devotion, learn this great lesson of the school of God : that it is good for us that men should not so much as know that we are in the world ; that we should live therein utterly unknown, or known only to be crucified, and to he held in utter contempt ; that there is nothing greater than to be trodden underfoot ; that the highest consolation is to suffer terrible crosses, both interior and exterior ; that everything in the world is nothing. Scarcely are directors to be met with who, esteeming no longer anything save God only and Jesus Crucified, and being intimately persuaded that there is nothing on earth—neither honours, nor pleasures, nor riches—which deserves to occupy the attention of a Christian, help souls to walk in the safe path of self-annihilation. If peradventure some are to be met with, instantly all hell conspires against them ; it excites a dread of them ; they are feared, no one knows why ; it causes a thousand rumours to be circulated about them ; it endeavours to create mistrust of them ; a thousand other directors or preachers do not alarm the devils so much as one of this sort. A devil, constrained by the authority of Holy Church, confessed that the person on earth he feared most was that holy man, Father John of the Cross, because, said this spirit of hell, he teaches men to go to God only by the road of nothingness ; accordingly, the effects of the rage of these diabolical spirits against the man of *God* were soon evident in the calumnies they raised against him, in the inquiries which superiors instituted into his life, and in the ill-treatment which he received at their hands.[1]

As the Cherubim are the sacred ministers of the light of God, so are the Seraphim of His love. Whoever, then, aspires to pure love, ought to feel an extraordinary love for these amiable spirits, and to cultivate a special intimacy with them. The saints who have excelled the most in pure love received marvellous aid from them ; as, for instance, St Francis and St Teresa. It was a Seraph, as we have already noticed, who imprinted on St Francis the Wounds of the Saviour ; it was a Seraph who lovingly pierced with a sacred arrow the generous heart of the great Teresa. All the great lovers of the Son of God, those who have excelled even among the greatest saints, can have no higher glory in Heaven than that of being placed in the choir of these spirits who are all love. It is to their blessed company that the souls most eminent in perfection may aspire. The late M. Gallemant, a most apostolic man, and one of the first superiors of the holy Order of the Carmelites in France, said that this Order was destined to fill up the choir of the Seraphim, if it made good use of the super-excellent grace it employs. In the miraculous apparitions with which the Blessed Virgin favoured the Venerable John of the Cross, this Queen of Angels was seen holding a casket, or, as it might be, a book, of marvellous whiteness, which rested on the head of a Seraph, and which she presented to St Teresa, and to this man of God, who was kneeling at her feet. Now this casket evidently signified the Carmelite rule; it was laid on the head of a Seraph, to intimate that they who were called to observe it were under obligation to live as Seraphim on earth ; and this Seraph appeared without a crown, because be represented those who are yet in the way ; above were to be seen others with their crowns on, to show at the same time that, after this life, these earthly Seraphim should share the crowns of the heavenly Seraphim, and fill the seats from which the apostate spirits of this choir were miserably precipitated.

Note

[1] See supra, p. 69.

FOURTH PRACTICE.

To Have a Great Devotion to St Michael, St Gabriel, St Raphael, and the four other Angels who are before the Throne of God.

It was St Michael who took up the defence of the honour of God against Lucifer, in the cause of the Incarnation of the Word;[1] and St John Chrysostom is of opinion, that he was also one of the first to pay his homage to Him in the crib of Bethlehem, on the day of His humble Birth. It is he who is the tutelary Archangel of the Church, and it is not without good reasons that he is believed to be the special guardian also of France. The signal aid which this kingdom has at times received from him is a strong proof of it. This great prince of Paradise has even chosen to have a place specially consecrated to him in this kingdom, within the diocese of Avranches, which at this day is popularly called Mont Saint-Michel, a place famous for the concourse of people who flock to it from all quarters, to honour this holy Archangel. It is he who assists souls at the dreadful hour of death, and who, according to the doctrine of St Augustine and St Bonaventura, not only assists them at that moment which decides their eternal lot, but also introduces them after death into Heaven. It is well here to remark, that he awaits the command of the august Mother of God to assist in a more especial manner those souls which she peculiarly favours : such is the opinion of St Bonaventura; and fitly, indeed, has the will of Heaven reserved this grace to the Queen of Heaven. Oh, how sweet it is to live and die under the protection of a patroness so loving and so worthy of love ! It is St Michael, in fine, who is held to be the first of all the angels in glory, and the most exalted of the Seraphim. If, then, we love the interests of God only, we must love him ; for he is the great saint of the cause of God, and of God Incarnate. If we love the Church, if we love ourselves, if we have any care for our salvation, if we desire to be succoured at the last moment of life, we must honour him greatly in all the necessities of the Church : for the destruction of schisms and heresies; for the establishment of ecclesiastical discipline in all its vigour ; for holiness of life in its prelates, and specially in the Sovereign Pontiff ; for the preservation and increase of the faith in those countries where it already exists ; and for the promulgation of the gospel in heathen lands.

St Gabriel is also one of the highest of the Seraphim, and when, like St Michael, he is styled an Archangel, we must not understand it to be meant thereby that he belongs only to the eighth choir of angels ; for this title of Archangel is common to all those who are highest in eminence among the princes of Heaven, just as the name of angel is applied indifferently to all these blessed spirits, of whatever order they may be, as well to the Seraphim as to the Angels of the ninth and lowest choir. It is St Gabriel who was chosen by God to negotiate the mystery of the Incarnation ; and those who believe that the Queen of Heaven had a special angel-guardian consider that it was to this glorious prince that the care of her was entrusted. And even according to the opinion of those doctors who think that the Mother of God had no angel-guardian, but was attended by troops of ministering angels, St Gabriel was one of the chiefs of these blessed bands appointed to serve her to whom a God did not disdain to subject Himself.

St Raphael is also one of the seven great princes who stand before the throne of the Divine Majesty, as Scripture teaches us (Tob. xii. 15) : on this point there is no room for doubt. We have but to read in Scripture of the services he rendered to Tobias, to love with a holy fervour this spirit of Heaven. It is hard, indeed, not to experience a sweet tenderness in one's heart at the recital of the charitable assistance which he gave him. When the father of Tobias sent him to the city of Rages, and enjoined him to seek a faithful guide to go with him on his journey, St Raphael appeared to him visibly under the form of a young man of great beauty, and accompanied him during his whole journey, consoling and instructing him, delivering him from great perils, and rendering him unnumbered services. At first meeting he salutes him, saying, "Joy be to thee always;" he delivers him from the sea monster who was about to devour him; he procures him wealth, and obtains for him a wife; he hinders the devils from injuring him; he restores sight to his father ; he bestows upon him and his whole family benedictions of heavenly peace, a joy of Paradise, and abundance of all good things, both for this life and the next. He conducted, as we have already observed, St Macarius the Roman during three years, in a visible form, far into the desert, having continued to bear him company from the time of his quitting Rome, whence he had fled, leaving his wife on the day of his marriage while the guests were dancing. He cured a novice of the Order of St Dominic from the falling sickness, on condition of his preserving perfect chastity. He delivered a French pilgrim who was on his road to St James of Compostella from the hands of robbers ; in fine, it needs only to be devout to him to experience the favours which he dispenses with a wonderful liberality.

There are four other princes of Heaven, beside St Michael, St Gabriel, and St Raphael, who are nearest to the throne of God, but whose names are not known with any certainty. Some, however, say that the fourth is named Uriel, and they ground their opinion on the Book of Esdras,[1] as do St Ambrose and St Bonaventura. Father de Barri relates that a church was dedicated to God in honour of these seven princes in the city of Palermo, the capital of Sicily ; that there was another in the city of Rome, which was consecrated by Julius III.; and that there was even a Confraternity established in honour of them in the afore-mentioned town of Palermo. He relates, moreover, that particular symbols have been appropriated to them by which painters might portray them, and that they may be seen admirably represented in the same city of Palermo, as well as at Antwerp and in other places. St Michael, treading Lucifer underfoot, bears in his left hand a green palm, and holds in his right a lance, at the end of which is a standard white as snow, with a crimson cross in the centre. St Gabriel appears with a torch inclosed in a lantern, which he holds in his right hand, the left being engaged in displaying a mirror of green jasper sprinkled with hues of divers colours. St Raphael is represented with a fish issuing from his mouth, holding in his left hand a box, and with his right leading the young Tobias. Uriel, or the fourth angel, bears in his hand a drawn sword, while the left, which hangs by his side, is enveloped in flames. The fifth has the bearing of a suppliant, with his eyes modestly cast down. The sixth has a golden crown in his right hand, and a scourge of three black thongs in the other. The seventh has at the edge of his mantle, which is folded over, a profusion of white roses. I have been led to describe these emblems of the angels in the hope that it may give some one the wish to have them painted ; for it is very certain that even the sight of pictures or images of angels inclines to purity and to heavenly love.

However, it is an assured truth that there are seven princes who stand before the God of all greatness, since Scripture teaches this ; and that they have a special power to assist men, since, at the beginning of the Apocalypse (i. 4), grace and peace are given in the name of these sublime Intelligences.

Nothing remains for us, then, but to honour them devoutly, and to implore their assistance in the ways of salvation. Self-love is our greatest enemy : now it has been revealed that St Michael is deputed by God to destroy it, as St Gabriel, in like manner, is appointed to establish the love of God. Here, then, are the two great points necessary to salvation : hatred of ourselves, and love of God. In order to attain to these, we must be rid of all sin, and have acquired the virtues. We must have recourse to these seven princes of Paradise, that they may obtain for us the grace to avoid the seven deadly sins, and may enrich us with the seven gifts of the Holy Spirit. Those who travel should often recommend themselves to St Raphael ; and, in the order of Providence, it appears that it is the will of God to employ this angel to assist pilgrims and wayfarers.

Notes

[1] It is a common opinion among divines that, on the mystery of the Incarnation being revealed to the angels before the creation of man, the pride of Lucifer, highest of all the heavenly host, revolted at the thought that human nature should be preferred before the angelic, and refused to do homage to the Sacred Humanity which was to be hypostatically united with the Divinity in the Person of the Son of Mary.

Contemplating his own perfections, and coveting the prerogatives of the Man-God, he said in his heart, "I will be like the Most High" (Isa. xiv. 14) : to which the glorious Archangel defiantly replied, *"Mi-cha-el—— Who is like God?"*

[1] 4 Esdras iv. 1. This book is not in the Canon of Scripture.

FIFTH PRACTICE.
To hold Interior Converse with the Holy Angels.

The life of the Christian is a spiritual life : if, then, we live in the spirit, why do we not walk and act in the spirit? We are raised to a supernatural state : being, then, in a condition so divine, ought we to live a life wholly sensual ? Woe to us who are immersed in flesh and blood ; who are like to the idols of the heathen *;* who have eyes and see not, ears and hear not ! We act like men devoid of faith ; this spiritual eye of our soul,—it is thus St Augustine describes faith,—remains inactive in us, and well-nigh utterly useless. We could scarcely be more attached to things of sense, or in a profounder forgetfulness of the interior world, if we lived amidst Pagan darkness. Ah, what heavenly beauties are discoverable in this spiritual world ! What magnificence, what wonders, what glory ! And it must be confessed that the holy angels shine therein conspicuously, and that, if our conversation, as the Apostle testifies (Phil, iii. 20), ought to be heavenly, we are under an obligation of conversing frequently with these amiable spirits of Heaven.

St Bernard, that devoted client of the angels, was truly of this opinion when, exhorting his brethren to be devout to these angelic spirits, he said, "Accustom yourselves, my dear brethren, to hold familiar conversation with the angels, and think often of them;" and what, indeed, are we thinking of when we bestow not a thought on these dazzling splendours of Paradise? O my God, Thy creatures here below love so much whatever is beautiful, and take such pleasure in contemplating it ; they have such difficulty in detaching themselves from it ; they are so ready to converse with those on earth who are amiable and attractive: and behold the world is full of angels of Paradise, since each man has his own, not to speak of so many others sent by God, and these angels are perfectly beautiful, and endowed with a marvellous power; the sweetness of their love for man is most attractive ; they possess all imaginable qualities which can inspire a holy love ; add to which, they are the princes and kings of the empyrean, and yet, alas ! scarcely any one thinks of them, and it is very rare to meet with persons who hold much converse with the angels. "Is it," says again the Saint whom I have just quoted, "that we doubt their presence, because we see them not ?" But ought we, then, to judge of the presence of things solely by our bodily eyes? Have men no souls, because we cannot see souls? Is God not everywhere, because our senses do not perceive His presence? It is because we have not faith, you will reply ; and this is true. We may add to this that it is also because we are too much attached to earthly things : let us, then, weep bitterly over our want of faith and our earthly attachments. The holy solitaries used to converse familiarly with the angels : it was because they lived an angelic life ; and we, miserable creatures that we are, can scarcely think of them for a quarter of an hour : it is because our life is altogether earthly.

Here is a practice tending to remedy this evil. A person standing at a window which opened upon a public thoroughfare, was struck with a ray of light which sensibly touched his heart : in this heavenly ray he discerned that men lived in an incredible oblivion of the world of grace. Penetrated with this truth, he set himself to listen to what the persons who were passing through the street were talking about; and he heard not one word of God, or of the things of God. No one spoke except of earth—of fine weather, of eating and drinking, of dress, of horses, and such like things. Oh, how many angels, he said to himself, are passing by here, accompanying these poor people ! Is it possible that not one among all this crowd is thinking of these princes of Paradise? This thought affected him much, and then he went to a neighbouring fair, with the object of paying his respects to the angels of the persons who were flocking thither in crowds from all quarters. He sighed when he beheld in so large a gathering so little attention paid to the numerous angels present there. He went from place to place in order to salute them and converse with them. Truly, he exclaimed to himself, here are far other sights to be seen than all the merchandise and rareties of the fair!

This practice is well worthy of our imitation. We are in some town, and are walking through the streets filled with people: Oh, why, then, do we not contemplate interiorly the angels who accompany all this multitude? Why do we not go out sometimes for the mere purpose of conversing with them? You enter a church, or some large assembly: Oh, why do you not raise yourself above the region of sense and contemplate all the holy angels present? You are travelling in company with others; you speak to them, you converse with them: why not also with their guardian angels?

I was told by a person who was given to these practices, that he took pleasure in counting the number of people be was in company with, so that he might know the number of angels who undoubtedly were present; and in course of time the All-Good God, desiring to encourage his devotion, rendered him on occasions as sensibly conscious of their presence as if he had beheld them with his bodily eyes. He told me that sometimes, even when seated at dinner, all of a sudden the angels made themselves known to him in a manner which he could not explain, but which was more evident to him than if they had formed part of the visible company. You are journeying along the road: all the villages you pass through contain as many angels as there are inhabitants. Alas! how many of the great lords of Heaven abide in all these places; and yet these poor country-people, far from thinking of them with devotion, are scarcely aware of the fact. Why, then, do you not pay your court to all these kings of the glorious Paradise? Know that the more they are neglected, so much the more will they favourably regard the honour you show them. There are many angels in these villages to whom no one will ever give a thought: if you should honour them, they will be constrained to make you some return; for, indeed, these blessed spirits do not know what it is to be unthankful, and are incomparable in their gratitude. You would be very glad to be honoured with the gratitude of some prince of the blood-royal, or of some of the great monarchs of this world. Why, then, do you not enter into the same sweet alliances with thousands and thousands of the kings of the heavenly court? You sometimes say that you would be glad, when on your journeys, to be cheered with the society of some pleasant companion: but can you, in truth, have anything sweeter or more agreeable than the conversation you may enjoy with these amiable Intelligences? You go into the country : why do you not choose certain times for conversing in spirit with the angels who are there? Why not retire sometimes into your garden, why not take a solitary walk, that you may profit by this favour?

But what do you say of the presence of your holy Angel Guardian ? Shall he be continually thinking of you, and will you scarcely ever think of him? Do you believe that a short prayer, morning and evening, is a worthy acknowledgment of the favours he bestows upon you ? I would have a serious answer to my question : in good truth, if one of the princes of the earth were to visit you, would you leave him from morning till night all alone, and think you acquitted yourself of your duty towards him if you made him an obeisance once or twice during the day—especially if all through the day he attended you everywhere, and rendered you all kinds of services ; while, on the other hand, you were yourself some poor disfigured wretch, foul with disease and corruption, loathed by all the world, yea, condemned to the gibbet for your crimes ? And suppose you were continually turning your back on this obliging prince, what astonishment would you create in those who might become acquainted with behaviour so grossly rude and contemptuous ! I ask you, moreover, whether your indignation is not excited at the mere imagination of such conduct? Tell me, do you feel yourself capable of it ? Oh, no : men are not insensible where earth is concerned, such insensibility is reserved for Heaven : for it is thus you treat the great prince of Heaven who is your guardian. O ye angels of Paradise, is it possible that you endure such insulting treatment ? It is most fitting, then, that we should converse with our angels; to leave them without a word would, indeed, be intolerable.

Choose, therefore, sometimes a quarter of an hour, half an hour, an hour, or more, and, retiring apart, converse at leisure with your good angel. Place yourself on your knees before him, prostrate yourself on the ground—for it is well to adopt this practice occasionally when alone ; ask his pardon for your ingratitude ; beg his holy benediction ; say all that a good heart would prompt one to say to a faithful and loving friend. Speak to him one while of your needs, of your miserable failings, of your temptations, of your weaknesses ; at another of Divine love, and of the holy ways which lead to God. Converse with him sometimes concerning the offences which men commit against their Sovereign, and concerning the divine interests of the Adorable Jesus and His most blessed Mother; at other times, consider in detail the obligations you are under to him, his goodness to you, his beauty, his perfections, his admirable qualities. Deal with him as with a kind father, as with a mother all tenderness, a true brother, an incomparable friend, a zealous lover, a vigilant pastor, a charitable guide, the witness of your most important secrets, a learned physician to heal all your sores, an advocate, and a powerful protector, a compassionate judge, a king entirely occupied with your welfare ; invoke him in all these characters, and in others which your love will suggest to you. They will serve you as so many considerations which will make you pass your time much more agreeably than with the creatures of earth.

We say that we are dull sometimes, that we have no one to speak to, and nothing to do : well, here is an occupation, here is something for us to do. A nun who had no relations, friends, or acquaintance to visit her, was asked whether, when she saw the other nuns receiving visits, she felt no regret. "Oh, no, indeed !" she replied, "for there is a very delightful person with whom I converse ; and when I hear that a sister is summoned to the parlour, forthwith I go and pay him a visit." And when her meaning was not understood, she led the way to an image of a holy angel that was in the convent : "Behold," she said, "my father and my mother, and all my kindred and acquaintance. Hither I come to converse, while my sisters are talking at the grate ; and I retire from my interview at least as well satisfied as they."

We ought also to go in spirit and visit heathen lands and heretical countries, to converse with all the angels of the inhabitants, so deplorably neglected; to mourn with them over the blindness and unbelief of these people; to speak to them of the kingdom of God, and to beseech them to labour for its establishment in all these nations. We may thus go the whole circuit of the earth, honouring successively and day by day the angels of each country: sometimes those of Canada, sometimes those of China, sometimes those of Japan, at other times those of the Indies; nor must we forget the angels of Christian kingdoms. It is also a very sweet occupation to ascend in spirit to the Heavenly Jerusalem, to converse for an hour sometimes with the Seraphim, at other times with the Cherubim, proceeding from choir to choir throughout the celestial hierarchies. What we have said may suggest matter for such conversations.

In fine, it is a very laudable practice to be in the habit of saluting the holy angels of those we meet. If we meet some great personage on our road, we salute him, as we do also any friend; and should we meet them a hundred times over, we do not fail to pay them this civility on each occasion. Is it fitting, then, that we should be so unmindful of the princes of Heaven, our truest friends? The thing is so easy; you would not have to make any more obeisances in consequence; all you need do is to make a good intention once for all, and enter into a solemn engagement, which you will take care to renew at least every week, that as often as you salute any one, you purpose at the same time to salute his holy angel. Whenever you remember it, you will, at the same time that you salute any one, secretly within yourself tell his holy angel that you salute him also. To this end, accustom yourself to see with the eyes of your mind the angels of those whom you behold with your bodily eyes; by degrees it will become very easy to you to remember the holy angels, and you will receive all sorts of blessings from them. When you enter a church, or any place where numbers are assembled, do not fail to salute all the angels present; and when you are in company with intimate friends, it will be well to say one to another aloud, "I salute your holy angel." I have seen the pious practice of which I speak solidly established through this means; so that it became the custom in a company, both on entering and departing, when mutual salutations were exchanged, to say aloud, "I salute your holy angel." Others, when writing to a friend, never neglect to conclude their letter with a salutation to the holy angel of the person whom they are addressing; sometimes even begging him in the name of both to salute the angels of the places where each resides. O my God! is not this what we do every day in regard to our miserable fellow-creatures? And why should we not at least pay the same respect to these favourites of Jesus and Mary?

It will be said that these are extraordinary devotions, and I confess they are so; but it must also be confessed that they ought to be very ordinary. It is an extraordinary thing to see a man or woman who is a true saint; it is an extraordinary thing to see even Christian families, in the very cities and towns of Christendom, in which the love of God reigns, and from which sin has been banished. Alas! all the world is immersed in the malice of sin; but is that a reason for exclaiming when we exhort persons to aim at what is therefore extraordinary? Must we be found fault with because we preach holiness, the love of God, and the destruction of sin? It is true that devotion to the holy angels is rare, that interior converse with these heavenly spirits is uncommon; but it is this very thing which we ought to lament with tears. In letters written by Turks, the name of Mahomet everywhere appears; and Christians who make an especial profession of piety will declaim against a letter in which the Name of God is frequently mentioned, or in which an attempt is made to show respect to the holy angels! At the end of the last century, that celebrated holy man, Father de Royas, confessor to Queen Margaret at the court of Spain, not only used openly to salute the courtiers with the words, "Ave, Maria," but even established this practice so firmly that the queen commonly saluted the king in like manner; and God was pleased to reward the devotion of this great queen, and to stamp this pious practice with His approbation, by a signal miracle performed in the person of this princess, upon occasion of her confessor saluting her with these holy words. That man of God used to place them at the beginning of all his letters, and, no doubt, he did not want for censurers in consequence—for some persons always disapprove of what they are not in the habit of doing themselves—but after his death, God plainly manifested, by the miracles with which He honoured him, that Heaven often bestows its approbation on what the men of this world condemn.

SIXTH PRACTICE.
To Perform Novenas in Honour of the Nine Choirs of Angels.

Catholics teach that we must not have a superstitious regard to numbers, and this is the doctrine of Holy Church; but we may also say, without superstition, that there are certain mysterious numbers consecrated by the piety of the faithful : as that of forty, which, the holy Fathers remark, was sanctified in the Person of our Lord, and in those of the ancient prophets ; that of three, which, being multiplied by three, forms the number nine, which represents to us the Most Holy Trinity ; this is why in Heaven there are three hierarchies of angels, and each hierarchy is composed of three choirs ; and it is amongst these nine choirs that the elect will be placed. Hence it is that the devotion of novenas has been popularised by the pious custom of the faithful ; and the seraphic St Teresa informs us that she practised this devotion, and performed numerous novenas in her various needs.

It is, then, a praiseworthy practice to perform novenas, and especially in honour of the nine choirs of angels, to which we have peculiar motives to excite us. I can bear witness to the extraordinary graces which have been the fruit of this devotion. I have seen marvellous things take place while the holy angels were being honoured by this exercise, and the power of the devils ruined in matters of serious importance ; and it is a most efficacious means for obtaining the assistance of Heaven in public calamities and private necessities.

We have already spoken at some length of the assistance which the holy angels render us in all our needs, whether bodily or spiritual, and we shall again recur to the subject in the course of this treatise. We have observed that, among these celestial bands, the Archangels and the Principalities ought to be particularly invoked for the welfare of kingdoms and provinces, and for those who rule them; and so, again, that the angels who have the more immediate care of the visible heavens, the elements, and seasons, ought to be invoked in time of war, pestilence, famine, and other public afflictions ; the Powers, against sorcerers, magicians, and their spells ; against the devils, their rage, and their malice ; the Virtues, for obtaining of an All-Merciful God extraordinary aid in our necessities, since it is these blessed spirits whom God often employs to work His wonders and miracles, according to the testimony of St Gregory, as we have already noticed. We refer the reader to what we have said concerning the nine choirs of angels in the first three chapters of this second treatise; and he can read on the vigil of each day of the novena so much as regards the choir which he intends to honour on the morrow.

We will here furnish some directions in a few words. Let the first day of the novena be devoted to honouring the angels of the lowest choir; we may ask of them faith, which is the beginning and the foundation of the spiritual life. On the second day we may venerate the Archangels, and ask of them zeal in the cause of Him whom faith makes known to us, begging that the same knowledge which comes of faith may be imparted to all unbelievers and heretics. On the third day the Principalities ; praying for the preservation and augmentation of faith in Catholic countries ; and, as faith ought to be accompanied with a good life, we will offer our prayers for the extirpation of sin and for the reformation of the inner man. On the fourth day we may honour the Powers ; invoking their aid against the might of those devils who war against us in the ways of faith, and counteract our designs of Christian mortification. On the fifth day, the Virtues; imploring their help to surmount the difficulties which the flesh and the world oppose to us in the paths of the spiritual life, and to obtain a holy generosity in the exercise of the Christian virtues. The sixth day may be given to the Dominations, in order that we may know the requirements of God, what He asks of us, and that His Divine will may be manifested to us. The seventh day to the Thrones, that they may obtain for us a perfect subjection and an entire abandonment to the will of God, wherein consists that peace which passes all imagination. The eighth day may be devoted to the Cherubim, for the establishment of the light of Jesus Christ in us, and a renunciation of all the maxims of the world opposed to it. The ninth day to the Seraphim, for the reign and triumph of pure love in our hearts.

The same devotion may be practised in time of public calamities, which come upon us and continue to afflict us because we fail to look sufficiently to their cause. We attribute them to this person and to that, while we ought to accuse ourselves and our own sins. God strikes us only that we may look to Him, whereas we keep our eyes always fixed on creatures. We ask for His peace, and we are ever fighting against Him ; our lives remain unchanged and our sins increase. Oh, how needful to us is the succour of the holy angels ! and how good it is to perform novenas in their honour, beseeching them to appease the just anger of God, and to labour for the destruction of sin, His cruel enemy, and for the ruin of all the plots of the powers of hell !

This devotion of novenas is also very profitable to us as a preparation for the due celebration of the feasts of our Lord and of His blessed Mother ; conversing each day with the angels of the choir we mean to honour, expressing to them our desire to love our gracious Master and our loving Mistress ; entreating them to supply our lack of love, and to thank Them, praise Them, and bless Them for us, and to obtain for us a solid devotion to Them, which may ever increase more and more.

Now, in order to perform these novenas well, every one can follow the attraction of grace and the advice of some good servant of God. However, to facilitate the practice, we will suggest that those who are able can have nine Masses celebrated in honour of the nine choirs of angels, burn nine candles, give nine alms; at least they can hear nine Masses with that intention, perform nine acts of mortification, whether exterior or interior, make nine genuflexions every day, recite the Angelical Salutation nine times, if they have not sufficient leisure to say nine Paters, a pious exercise, which, it may be remarked, was revealed by Heaven to St Mecthilde; they can visit nine times some chapel or altar dedicated to God in honour of the holy angels, or the altar where the Blessed Sacrament reposes, and where the princes of God's court attend upon Him. Besides this, they can communicate according to the advice of their director ; place themselves on their knees three times a day, in the morning, about noon, and in the evening, prostrating themselves before the angels of the choir which they mean to honour particularly that day ; and during the course of the day they may address to them many ejaculatory prayers, and endeavour to converse for some space of time with these spirits of love. If several persons should unite together, they would draw down more abundant benedictions : in this case each can choose a day to visit some church, or some poor persons, and, if possible, to fast, so that a perpetual fast may be maintained during the whole of the novena.

SEVENTH PRACTICE.

To take Certain Days every Month and every Week for the Purpose of Honouring more especially the Holy Angels, and to Celebrate their Feasts with all Possible Devotion.

I know of a holy community of Carmelite nuns, where every month they select one of the nine choirs of the holy angels to pay it peculiar honour; and as three months remain of the twelve in the year, these three months are devoted to some one of the choirs towards which they feel more peculiarly drawn ; as, for instance, that of the Seraphim. My dear readers, it is in your power to do the very same thing; the practice is an easy one.

If yon like, you can choose the first nine days of each month to pay your respects to these angelic spirits, and then select some other days for invoking those angels to whom you are specially indebted ; or, if you have the good will to undertake it, you might apply yourself on Sundays to honour the Seraphim, Cherubim, and Thrones; on Mondays, the Dominations, the Virtues, and the Powers : on Tuesdays, the Principalities, Archangels, and Angels ; on Wednesdays, the angels of unbelievers and heretics; on Thursdays, the angels of kingdoms and provinces, of churches and altars, and specially those who attend on our Divine King in the Most Holy Sacrament ; on Fridays, the angels of your enemies, or of such persons as are a cause of trouble to you, or from whom you have reason to apprehend some injury ; on Saturdays, the angels of your relatives and friends, and of those with whom you most frequently associate ; if you belong to a community, of those with whom you live, particularly your spiritual friends and your director. These angels take much greater interest in your welfare than you imagine. Do not forget the angels of the town or village where you reside.

As for the angel who is your guardian, every day of your life ought to be a day of devotion to him, and of thanksgiving for his marvellous goodness to you. Some set apart their birthday as an especial festival in his honour, doing exactly as they would upon the festivals of those saints to whom they have the greatest devotion, both in the way of preparation and in keeping the octave. In addition, those whose circumstances permit of it, give as many alms in his honour as they have lived years, or else make as many acts of some virtue, or offer as many acts of devotion to their amiable guardian.

I knew a person who used at such times to distribute the years of his life over several days, in order to consider at leisure the mercies of God towards him ; the misfortunes from which he had been preserved or delivered, whether affecting body or soul ; the graces he had received from the infinite goodness of the Adorable Jesus; the protection of the most holy Virgin, and that of the angels and saints. Such considerations powerfully touch the heart when they are well made ; and as our holy angel is the minister whom God employs to shield us from all evil, and to convey to us His benefits, this furnishes full occasion to thank him and to bless him in detail for all his loving care in our youth, in more advanced years, and in our old age, if we have attained it, carefully calling to mind the principal things which have occurred to us in the course of our life. We ought at least to remember that Tuesday is a day dedicated to the honour of the holy angels ; and this day ought to be one of great devotion with such as love them. The twenty-ninth of September is the day of the great feast of St Michael and of all the other angels. The eighth of May is the feast of his Apparition on Mount Garganus. And in Normandy the sixteenth of October is observed in commemoration of the Apparition of this glorious Archangel on the Hill of Tombe, commonly called Mont Saint-Michel.

This place is very famous owing to the concourse of persons who flock to it from all quarters to pay their homage to this amiable prince of Heaven; and the great miracles which the Omnipotence of God has worked there are prevailing motives to excite the devotion of the faithful more and more to honour on this holy hill the God of all mercy, and to implore the succour of the highest prince in His heavenly court. Pilgrimages may be undertaken to this holy spot for every manner of need, but especially for deliverance from the temptations and assaults of the malignant spirits, and to obtain purity of mind and body and an invincible fortitude in the ways of salvation. Those who are devoted to the interests of our Lord Jesus Christ and His most holy Mother, ought to address themselves to this glorious Archangel, who so zealously maintained Their cause from the very beginning of the world; it would be desirable, however, that persons should perform this pilgrimage with more devotion than is usually seen, conversing together of God as they journey along, raising their hearts often to our Lord and to His most holy Mother, imploring the aid of St Michael, St Gabriel, St Raphael, and all the nine choirs of angels ; being very watchful to avoid all manner of sin ; and finally, on reaching their destination, not neglecting to confess and communicate. A voice from Heaven made known that this place is very agreeable to God and frequented by holy angels. Truly such an oracle must serve to soften any hardships which may be incurred in visiting this sacred mount ; and it is sweeter than words can express, or the imagination can conceive, to find one's self in a spot so dear to God and the constant resort of the princes of His court.

Divine Providence has even ordered that it should not be any man of this earth, however holy, but a pure spirit of Heaven, and the highest of all the blessed spirits, who should consecrate the church; for St Aubert, Bishop of Avranches, when about to perform that ceremony, was prevented by St Michael, who apprised him that he himself had already consecrated it. This is the holy bishop to whom the Archangel appeared on three several occasions, more than nine hundred years ago, to inform him that the Hill of Tombe was under his protection and that of all the other angels ; and that it was the will of God that a church should be built in their honour. On the third occasion he touched the good bishop's head, and left thereon a mark which is visible to this day.[1] An admirable prodigy likewise occurred, for a rock, which stood there, proving an impediment to the convenient erection of the sanctuary of the church, the Archangel directed that an infant still in its cradle should be brought to the spot, and on the child touching the rock with its foot, immediately it fell and left the necessary space for the sanctuary. Blessed are the chaste and the innocent, the pure and clean of heart, since they are so dear to God and to His angels !

St Michael, not content with working all these wonders, and desiring to bestow still greater visible tokens of his favour upon the holy Mount of Tombe, commanded St Aubert to send to Mount Garganus, and ask, in his name, for a portion of the vermilion cloth which he had left there, and for a fragment of the marble on which he was seated when he appeared on that mountain in human form ; which being granted at the request of the good bishop's deputies, twelve blind persons, at different places, received their sight by touching these holy things; and near the Mount of Tombe a blind woman also had her sight restored, whereat the people were so deeply moved, that, in memory of so great a miracle, the village, which had been heretofore called Astériat, was named Beauvoir, and so it is called at this present day. I enjoyed the honour and the blessing of beholding, in this very year 1667, on the day of the feast of the Apparition of the glorious St Michael, at this sacred spot, these precious tokens of the incomparable love of this great prince of Paradise for men, as also the shield and the sword which are preserved there in the treasury of the church, and which are additional proofs of his marvellous goodness. The shield is adorned with little crosses, and its material is brass, as is that also of the sword ; these are also gifts of the Archangel, which he made on the occasion of a miracle wrought in Great Britain by his invincible strength, and which he commanded to be brought to this place.

History relates that there was a dragon there of a monstrous size, who, poisoning the waters with his venom, infecting the air with his breath, and killing every one he met, had rendered the country around almost uninhabitable. This affliction constrained the bishop of the place to have recourse to God ; and, after having proclaimed a three days' fast, and given abundant alms, all the inhabitants armed themselves and marched, accompanied by the clergy, who walked in procession, imploring the succour of Heaven to give strength to the people to destroy the dragon ; but great was their astonishment when, having nearly reached the place of his retreat, they found him dead, with the aforementioned shield and sword lying by him ; and while they were wondering who it was that had been able to kill this monster with such feeble weapons, St Michael appeared to the bishop, and told him that it was he who had slain the dragon; and that, although he needed not those weak arms to effect his purpose, yet he had been pleased to make use of them, that he might leave visible tokens of the assistance he had rendered. He then commanded these arms to be carried to the church on the Mount of Tombe, where they are still preserved with singular veneration.

Since it has pleased God, about three years ago, to manifest anew in our days the great St Gaudentius, Bishop of Evreux, through the discovery of his holy body five leagues from Mont Saint-Michel, it has appeared to me that our Lord would be glorified if, when speaking of the miracles He has wrought to the glory of the angels on the Mount of Tombe, I said a word of those He works at this present time near that holy hill in honour of this truly angelic man. Entirely given to God, having no longer about him anything of this earth, and seeming to breathe only the air of Paradise, he voluntarily resigned the government of the see of Evreux, and quitted the society of men that he might converse only with the angels in solitude. Having left, then, his dear flock, who accompanied him for the distance of two leagues from the town of Evreux to a spot where, in memory of this last farewell, a holy chapel was built in honour of the Blessed Virgin, who is the special Lady and Patroness of this diocese, and in honour of St Michael, which chapel is commonly called Nôtre Dame de Gaud, this great prelate retired into a solitary district near Granville, on the sea shore, five leagues, as we have said, from Mont Saint-Michel, where, having ended his days and left his precious relics, God, who delights in manifesting those who hide themselves for the love of Him, was not contented with glorifying him at the period of his holy death, but five hundred years afterwards made known his glory by the first invention of his body, which was there found perfectly uncorrupted, and was suffered to remain in the sepulchre where he had been interred. Many miracles occurred at that time, and it became a place of resort for afflicted persons; but in the lapse of ages, about five hundred years and more after this first invention, it pleased Divine Providence to reveal once again the greatness of this saint by the second invention of his relics about three years ago, followed in like manner by many miracles ; on which account the place has become very famous, and a most favourable spot for those who desire to implore the intercession of St Gaudentius. I should be most ungrateful were I not to publish the help I myself received from this great saint, in a dangerous illness, when the physicians had pronounced my case to be hopeless. Blessed for ever be God for His great mercies, which He never ceases to bestow on men through the merits of His most blessed Mother, His angels, and His saints. Near the tomb of St Gaudentius is that of St Paternus, Bishop of Avranches, and of the Abbot St Scubilion, who were his companions in his retreat. St Senator is also buried there, as well as many other holy persons. Remains are still visible of the hermitages of these saintly recluses.

The feast of St Gabriel is celebrated on the eighteenth of March, and in some places on the twenty-fourth of the same month, the vigil of the feast of the sacred Mother of God. That of St Raphael is kept on the twentieth of November, and in some places on one of the Sundays occurring between Easter and Pentecost That of the Guardian Angels is solemnised on the first day of October not occupied by a feast of nine lessons, and it is also celebrated on the first day of March. All these ought to be great days with such as are devout to the holy angels. They should hear Mass and communicate in honour of them; practise some mortification or do some work of charity; but besides this, at least for one, if not for more, of these feasts special preparation ought to be made. St Francis used to fast forty days to prepare himself for the feast of St Michael; and it was during this quarantine that a Seraph imprinted on him the sacred stigmata. St Elisabeth used to observe the same practice, fasting on bread and water. I have already spoken of St Mecthilde, who, having asked our Lord what she could do to honour the angels, He replied, "Daughter, you will say the *Pater* nine times in honour of their nine choirs." To these she added nine more in honour of her good angel, that he might present this her devotion to these glorious spirits. A preparation for their festivals might be made by a novena, according to the manner indicated in the last chapter. Moreover, we must not forget to keep their octaves, performing each day some pious duty towards these princes of Heaven.

Care should be taken to recite the offices and litanies of these holy spirits, at least on certain days, and at certain times of the year. There is a rosary which can be said in honour of our holy angel-guardian. At the cross we say the *Credo*, or the *Te Deum*, followed by the *Paternoster* and the *Ave Maria* ; then upon the large beads, either the *Gloria Patri* or the *Ave Maria;* and upon all the little beads, the *Angele Dei;*[1] or those who do not know the short prayer, may say the words, "My good angel, I love thee, and desire to love thee." If we wish to say it in honour of all the nine choirs, we may make use of these other words : "Holy angels, I love you, and desire to love you." The use of ejaculatory prayers is wonderfully profitable. If you love the heavenly spirits you will often converse with them, and pour forth your heart in their presence ; nothing can be easier to a heart that loves than to tell them of its grief for the ingratitude of men, its astonishment at the forgetfulness in which they live of their perfections and their goodness ; nothing easier than to express its own gratitude for their care, and its desire to profit by it ;

nothing easier than to call them to our assistance in our necessities, and to beseech them to interest themselves for us with Jesus and Mary, in order to render Them favourable to us, to say to Them what we would desire to say, but alas ! are not able. We understand nothing of the language of the court of Paradise ; and we need the intervention of these princes of the court to speak for us. We may express all this during the course of the day in two or three fervent words, sometimes in one way, and sometimes in another.

I had almost forgotten to mention a practice which will enable you to keep a festival, sometimes to one angel, and sometimes to another. With this view you must form the intention, when you keep the feast of any saint, to keep, at the same time, that of the holy angel who was his guardian here below. This will not multiply your devotions : you have only to make the intention of honouring the holy angel of the saint by all the good works you shall perform in the saint's honour, and by this means you will spend the whole year in keeping the feasts of different angels. You will thus lay an obligation on the saints to offer your homage to these glorious spirits, to whom they are so greatly indebted ; you will gain the favour of all these angels, and will draw down upon yourself the sweetest benedictions of Paradise.

Notes

[1] The cathedral of Avranches, as is well known, was levelled to the ground, not one stone being left upon another, and all its sacred treasures scattered to the winds, by the impious revolutionists of the last century.

[1] "Angele Dei, qui custos es mei, me tibi commissum pietal© superna illumina, custodi, et guberna."

"Angel of God, who art my guardian, enlighten, guard, direct, and govern me, who have been committed to thee by the divine mercy."

The above prayer is indulgenced.

EIGHTH PRACTICE.

To Visit Churches and Oratories Dedicated to God in Honour of the Holy Angels.

The heretics, to whom all piety is odious, blame pilgrimages, which the Holy Catholic Church approves, and holds in such high estimation, that the Sovereign Pontiff, who is its head, even when granting other faculties, often reserves to himself the power of dispensing with vows to perform pilgrimages to Rome, Jerusalem, and St James of Compostella. God sufficiently marks the favour with which He regards such devotions, by attaching so many graces and especial favours to these places which He does not bestow elsewhere. We may, it is true, and we ought to have recourse to His fatherly kindness, and implore the protection of the most holy Virgin, and of the angels and saints, in all places, and in all churches and chapels whatsoever; but it cannot be denied that there are certain localities which this God of Mercy honours with miracles, which He does not do elsewhere; testifying by these tokens of a power and goodness extraordinary His approbation of the devotion of the pilgrims who flock thither from all quarters. We have saints, recognised as such in the Catholic Church, who spent the greater part of their lives in this kind of devotion; and the great Archbishop of Milan, St Charles Borromeo, had such a high esteem for it that, laden as he was with important affairs, and encountering, as he failed not to do, the contradiction of persons of the most exalted rank, he undertook many pilgrimages, and those long and arduous ones, under circumstances of no little difficulty. The church of Mount Garganus, dedicated to God in honour of St Michael, is one of those celebrated places to which pilgrims resort from all parts; and Otho III., Emperor as he was, walked to it barefoot from the city of Rome, although the distance is very great.

But as there are few who are able to make such long journeys, we may, as a substitute, pay a devout visit to some chapel or altar dedicated in honour of this prince of the heavenly hosts, or of the other holy angels. For some years past it has pleased our Lord to reawaken in men's hearts devotion to these blessed spirits in the city of Rouen, the capital of Normandy ; for which purpose He inclined the hearts of a number of devout persons to go every month and visit a chapel which is built upon a high hill, in the neighbourhood of that great city, in honour of the Archangel St Michael. This is how the thing occurred, as I have been informed :—Two or three servants of God, while performing their devotions in a celebrated church, where the most holy Virgin is invoked under the title of Nôtre Dame de Bon Secours, felt themselves moved to go and pray at the door of the aforenamed chapel of St Michael, which is at no great distance. They were greatly affected at seeing it in such an abandoned condition, although it had formerly been the object of great devotion, as is evident from the testimony of ancient writers, and from the mere inspection of what still remains of a road leading to it, paved with large stones, which must have been constructed with much cost and labour. They immediately resolved to repair to the spot from time to time, and some other persons to whom they communicated their plan entered readily into it. Now it has pleased the God of All Goodness to bestow so great a blessing on this devotion that, in the course of a few years—for, indeed, it is only recently begun—such multitudes have visited this chapel on the day chosen at the beginning of each month, as to make it requisite to have the sermon preached outside the building; and a touching sight it is to behold all this crowd modestly seated on the summit of the hill, and listening in deep silence to the discourse pronounced in praise of the holy angels ; for a preacher is always secured for every month, and the Holy Mass celebrated, at which numbers communicate. This devotion having been suggested in consequence of a visit to Nôtre Dame de Bon Secours, we have good reason to believe that it was a favour bestowed by this Queen of Angels, and a signal effect of her "good help."

Another devotional practice I have witnessed elsewhere ; which is that at the approach of the feast St Michael, or at the beginning of March, persons are deputed to go during nine days and pay their respects to the holy angels in one of the chapels dedicated to them; and sometimes nine persons acquit themselves each day of this duty, not to mention many others who go and offer their prayers every morning and evening ; every day the Holy Sacrifice of the Mass is celebrated, and nine tapers are kept burning.

NINTH PRACTICE.

To place great Confidence in the Protection of the Holy Angels, and to have Recourse to them in all our Neckssities, Bodily and Spiritual.

"They that trust in the Lord shall be as Mount Sion ; he shall not be moved for ever that dwelleth in Jerusalem. Mountains are round about it : so the Lord is round about His people" (Ps. cxxiv. 1, 2). Now, these mountains, which serve as impregnable bulwarks and fortresses to the soul which places all its hopes in the God of mercies, are none other than the holy angels ; these are the holy mountains of the Psalmist (cxx. 1), whence he looked confidently for help. Oh, how blessed is that soul which lives under such protection ! It shall be delivered from the snare of the hunters ; it shall not be afraid of the terror of the night ; the arrow that flieth in the day shall not hurt it, nor the plottings of darkness, nor the noon-day devil. While a thousand fall on its right hand, and ten thousand on its left, it shall abide in safety, because it is in the keeping of the angels. It shall walk upon the asp and the basilisk ; it shall trample under foot the lion and the dragon, and shall receive no injury (Ps. xc. 3-13). Its abode is so sure and lofty that evil cannot approach it; it shall fly like the eagles in mid-air without fear, and shall take its flight to the height of heaven, borne up by these glorious celestial powers. Whether it go or come, the angels accompany it as its guard; these are the warriors of whom the prophet Zacharias speaks (ix. 8), who encompassed the house of the Lord; they shall keep it in the midst of them, as heretofore they kept the heroic Machabeus, and will cover it on every side with their arms, rushing on its adversaries, and casting darts and tremendous fire-balls at all its enemies (2 Mach. X. 29, 30).

"Why, then, should we fear," exclaimed St Bernard, "seeing that we have friends so faithful, wise, and powerful?" "Joy be to thee always," said St Raphael the Archangel to Tobias (v. 11, 15); "I will conduct thee and bring thee back." And, truly, I do not see how we ever can be sad, being assisted in all our ways by such powerful help. If monsters should come up to devour us, our faithful guardians will easily deliver us out of their jaws. Let all hell conspire against us, let all mankind take up arms to destroy us, our hearts ought to fear nothing, if the choirs of angels grant us their protection. How sweet to think of this multitude of angels of whom we have spoken in the first treatise of this little work, and to know that all are engaged in the service of men! Whithersoever, then, I may go, and in whatever place I may find myself, I have thousands of millions of these soldiers of Heaven watching to defend me. O my soul! why art thou troubled? Why all this anxiety? Seest thou not that all Heaven is fighting for thy salvation? It seems to thee sometimes that thou art lonely and forsaken, deprived of all human succour; but why dost thou not remember that thou hast around thee an army of terrible might, composed of an innumerable multitude of invincible warriors, who accompany and protect thee? While we sleep there are more eyes open to watch over our safety than there are stars in the firmament. Though all the creatures on earth should rise up against us on every side, yet are there more angels of Paradise to defend us than there are atoms in the sun's rays and drops of water in the ocean.

Let us say, then, O my soul! We have more with us than our adversaries have with them. But oh, the blindness of men! Nothing affects us but what we behold with the eyes of flesh. We are feelingly alive to the presence of earthly creatures, as we are also to their withdrawal; when we see a good number on our side, or standing against us, our poor hearts expand with joy or contract with sadness; in vain are we reminded of the succours of Heaven: it is a language of which we understand nothing—in this resembling the servant of Eliseus, who, beholding the numerous array of picked and veteran troops sent by the king of Syria to capture his master, could not be reassured by anything the holy prophet could say to dispel his fears. In vain did he tell him that they had more with them for their defence, this poor man gave heed to nothing but what he saw; the invincible bands of the God of Hosts failed to encourage him, because they were not visible to him—herein how different from the man of God, who acted by faith, and whose confidence St Ambrose has so highly extolled, exclaiming at the thought of it, "Oh, the faith of the holy prophet! He fears not his enemies whom he sees, because he knows that the angels of God are with him, although he sees them not. But oh, the goodness of God! The holiness of a man," adds this Father, "draws more defenders down to him from Heaven than the malice of men raises up adversaries to him on earth." What need have we in the midst of our darkness to betake ourselves to prayer, like that holy man, when he perceived his servant's want of faith, and to say with him, "O Lord, open our eyes not to obtain a miracle, and to have mountains full of horses and chariots of fire disclosed to us, but to increase our faith, and make us live by it, and act always by this same virtue.

I must declare that I am perfectly astonished when I reflect upon the little confidence which men place in the protection of Heaven. "Oh, the avarice of the human heart!" said our Lord once to St Teresa: it feels as if the very ground were slipping from under it. Everywhere there is nothing but anxiety, as in temporal things so in spiritual. Men could not be more attached to human means if there were no Providence. But how sad it is to behold spiritual persons, under the pretext of prudence, so immersed in solicitude about everything that concerns them, and placing so much reliance on their own diligence. Oh, the accursed prudence of the flesh! I hold thee in eternal abhorrence. O loving Providence of my God! I abandon myself without reserve into Thy hands. Let men say and do what they will, let them combine against us as much as they please, I know, O my God—I know it without a shadow of doubt—I know it with more certainty than I know that I am writing these lines—that in spite of all the efforts and all the rage of devils, Thy divine counsels shall be accomplished. He whom Thou wiliest to save shall never be lost, unless he wills it himself; in vain may men cast him down, when they think that he will never rise again—then it is that Thou wilt render him more glorious. Thou raisest him from the dust and mire of the earth, from the dunghill to which his humiliations had abased him, to make him sit with the princes of Thy people, and to give him a throne of glory. Oh, who is like unto Thee, who inhabitest the Heavens, and lookest down from Thy sanctuary with favour upon the meanest things of the earth, putting down the mighty from their seat, and exalting the humble? Full well dost Thou manifest what Thou art, as is written of Thee in the Book of Wisdom (xvi. 8-10); giving death to the enemies of Thy people, and putting their adversaries to flight by the bitings of flies, whilst Thou givest victory to Thy children and to all Thy servants, whom not even the teeth of venomous serpents could overcome.

Let us, then, turn all our thoughts to the Lord, and commit all our cares to His Divine Providence, who watches over us by His holy angels with ineffable goodness. Let us lift up our hands and our eyes towards these holy mountains in all places and on all occasions. I have sufficiently shown the powerful help we receive from them both in spiritual and in temporal matters; and I will here only add to what has been already said, that on a thousand occasions angels have appeared in visible form to bring miserable sinners to the confession of their sins, and to the sacrament of penance. They have often administered the Most Holy Sacrament of the Altar: as to St Onuphrius, to whom they carried it every eight days in the desert. They assist in great numbers at the Holy Sacrifice of the Mass, as St Nilus testifies; and he relates that St John Chrysostom saw them diligently assisting the priests when they were giving communion to the people. They sometimes make responses at Holy Mass, as occurred in the case of St Oswald, the bishop. They join with men in their prayers, and recite them with them, as happened to the great St Ouen, Archbishop of Rouen, who had a singular devotion to the most holy Virgin, their Queen; for this holy man having commenced a verse of a Psalm in the church of St Peter at Rome, he heard the angels finishing it. Sometimes they show to those who fight for Jesus Christ the glorious crowns which are prepared for them.

When a heart experiences some difficulty in giving itself perfectly to God only, it need but address itself to them. St Ignatius found the advantage of it ; and it was the means he employed to gain St Francis Xavier; thus it is to these glorious spirits that Japan owes her apostle. The holy Order of the Carmelites has given to our own France souls admirable for their saintliness ; and here again it is to the holy angels to whom we are indebted ; for St Michael, the highest of these sublime Intelligences, appeared in complete armour, like a warrior returning from battle, to the Venerable Anne de Saint-Barthélemi, when the resolution was taken of bringing these holy virgins from the kingdom of Spain into France, notwithstanding all the opposition of hell ; this archangel desiring thereby to make known the victory he had gained over the demons, and over the obstacles which men had opposed. In fine, our Lord, by employing the ministry of angels at His Birth, during His Life, after His Death, and at His Ascension, teaches us that in all our actions and in all our ways we ought to have recourse to them, and implore their assistance.

Note

[1] 4 Kings vi. 15.

TENTH PRACTICE.

To Labour for the Conversion of Souls, and for their Relief in the Flames of Purgatory, in Honour of the Holy Angels.

What can we do more agreeable to the angels than to labour with them for the establishment of the glory of our common Master? It is with a view to this glory that the countless host of pure spirits is occupied with watching over miserable mortal creatures with such attention; it is this which, according to the Apostle, detains them all in the service of men. He who knows God can consider nothing mean when it is question of His Divine interests ; and if it is difficult to comprehend the charity, the patience, and the diligence of angels in serving such vile creatures as we are, let us cease to wonder when we consider that it is the glory of their Sovereign which makes them do and bear such amazing things. The least degree of God's glory, the very shadow of His interests, is worth the sufferings of the whole universe and the annihilation of all creatures. O my God! why art Thou not known? Truly our earth is the land of forgetfulness as to all Thou art and all that is due to Thee. It is impossible to think of this without experiencing a longing desire to leave it with all speed, in order to enter the land of light, where we shall perceive, although late, that we ought to have forgotten all things, or to have thought of them only for Thy sake.

Let us, then, with the holy angels, have regard to the interests of God in souls; and let us use all our endeavours that our Sovereign may be glorified in them. A God-Man having given His life amidst an accumulation of unspeakable torments for this end, we must either renounce our Christianity or give all that in our degree we can give to promote His glory in them. Tears of bitter grief ought to stream from our eyes at the sight of what passes around us. What expense is lavished in pampering and adorning a wretched body which every day is hastening to corruption, for the gratification of ambition and vanity! What revenues are every year squandered, what immense sums expended, throughout this earth on that which is nothing but earth! Consider for a moment what profit the men now living will derive from all this expenditure a hundred years hence, and take and meditate a while seriously on this truth. Then let us be lost in astonishment at beholding the small share which the interests of God have in all this outlay. Let us be plunged in an abyss of grief at seeing even those goods which are consecrated solely to the honour of God, the very revenues of the Church, employed—rather let us say squandered away—for every other purpose. Be rent asunder, O ye heavens, and be astounded at the fearful blindness and hardness of the hearts of Christians. In a report concerning Greece which was printed and distributed in the chief places of Christendom, it was stated that an annual revenue of a thousand crowns would suffice to maintain all the necessary missions in that country, and I know not whether throughout all Christendom the sum could be collected. O Christians ! it is question of winning new empires to Jesus Christ and to His Blessed Mother: I repeat it, new empires—alas ! what will not men do to conquer a single town?—by contributing something towards the foreign missions in the Indies, in China, in Japan, in Canada ; and yet you remain unmoved !

Nearly all our country places are made desolate by the reign of sin, and ignorance of our holy mysteries ; a small sum spent in giving missions would do much in the way of remedy; but there are very few who trouble themselves about the matter. So it is : money is forthcoming in abundance for a handkerchief, for a drees, for play, for horses, for furniture, for plate, for keeping dogs ; it is only when the interests of my God are concerned that no money is to be had, and nothing can be done. O Christians ! do you, in truth, know what you are doing? And ye holders of benefices, how can you live in peace, how can you take a moment's rest, beholding your houses filled with such handsome furniture, fine pictures, and magnificent plate, and the other expenses in which you indulge out of the patrimony of the poor? If you were to take twenty sous from a poor man, nay, but ten sous, to go and make merry with, what would you say ? what would others say? If you were to go and take a crown out of the poor-box in the church to spend upon your pleasures, or if you were to help yourselves to the same sum out of the offertory, would you not feel somewhat uneasy in your mind ? And yet every year you take from the poor and from churches sums of money beyond what your necessities require to a fearful amount ; you have, besides, much hoarded up ; and you keep all these splendid sideboards of plate, these pictures, which have been bought with this money ; and perhaps you will die in this state, without making restitution, leaving these things to your heirs, and thus pillaging the property of churches and of the poor even after your death : and all this while you laugh, and pass your days without fear. Oh, horror and desolation ! Verily, my God, I see the truth of those words of Thine, that few indeed are saved.

The example of the holy angels is a motive of wonderful power, not only to do all and to give all to promote the glory of God in souls, but also never to grow weary in so doing, nor be discouraged by the sufferings we have to endure. The Apostle teaches us (2 Tim. iv. 2), that we must instruct souls "with all patience and doctrine." These few words include everything: to say all patience and doctrine is to except neither suffering, nor contempt, nor toil, nor any form of instruction, whether in public or in private, whether by preaching or by catechising. Alas! the angels are ever thinking of us, though we scarcely ever think of them; they are constantly attending on us, notwithstanding the repulses and disregard with which we repay them. After offending God during the whole course of our lives, which is greatly to offend them also, they continue nevertheless to do us good, their love always triumphing over everything. This is why St Ignatius proposed them as an example to his children, in order to encourage them when they saw no fruit from their labours. And truly all our fervour is like ice, compared with the bright flames of pure love with which these spirits are animated. Where will you find the director, the preacher, who, after giving hundreds of counsels for years together, and receiving nothing in return but insults, will continue to proffer them with the same amiability? and yet the angels persevere with an unalterable fidelity after forty or sixty years, after thousands of millions of inspirations which they have given us. They see clearly that numbers of unbelievers and heretics of whom they have the charge are on the road to hell, and that all their endeavours will prove ineffectual; but this does not prevent their watching lovingly over them to the very last breath of life. Again we ask, where is the gardener who would continue diligently watering a tree if he knew that it would never bear fruit? But the goodness of the angels is beyond all compare. All directors, preachers, confessors, missionaries, and all such as labour in any way for the good of their neighbour, ought to have a special devotion to them, that they may in some measure participate in their charity and indefatigable patience.

As the care which these immortal spirits bestow upon us extends beyond time and after death, they may also be imitated in this persevering love. We shall give them much pleasure by assisting those departed souls who are burning in the fires of Purgatory; and they experience a special consolation when they behold us disposed to relieve them. Help, then, these poor souls by the Holy Sacrifice of the Mass, by mental and vocal prayer, by bestowing alms and visiting the poor for their intention, by fasts and mortifications, and by the indulgences which can be applied to them. If you possess a blessed medal, ascertain what indulgences are attached to it which are applicable to the dead ; to this end, procure the little book which contains a list of them, and have frequent recourse to this treasury in behalf of those poor souls. As there are many indulgences attached to medals—I speak of such as are common, and may be applied to the dead by the person who wears them; as, for instance, by reciting the *Pater* and *Ave* five times in honour of the Five Wounds of our Lord, or the *Pater* and *Ave* three times in honour of the Most Holy Trinity, before an image of our Lord or of our Lady—it will be easy for you to give some relief to these much afflicted souls several times a day.

I know persons who never omit this practice when in church, who never lie down to sleep without performing this act of devotion; and it is an easy thing to do, because all that is required is to wear one of these medals, and a picture of our Lord and of His Blessed Mother may readily be found in all Hours and Breviaries, and other pious books, when there happens to be none in the room we occupy, which, however, ought never to be. I know some persons who pass a considerable time in repeating these prayers over and over again, in order to obtain the more for these souls who are the prisoners of Divine justice ; for let us suppose, for instance, that the remission of a hundred days' penalty, or of ten years' penalty, were attached to each repetition of these prayers, we should relieve them of many years of suffering if we were to continue to repeat them devoutly for half an hour or an hour. I know persons who, when they desire to obtain something from God, endeavour to move Him to mercy by first performing this act of mercy themselves.

Ah ! if a dog had fallen into the fire you would feel compassion for him ; if a house were burning, every one would run for water to extinguish the flames; neither darkness nor bad weather would keep people back; crowds would hurry eagerly to the spot : whereas such is the prodigious blindness of Christians, a thing of ordinary occurrence in all spiritual concerns, that souls made to the image of God are enduring the torments of burning—your father, your mother, your husband, your wife, your dearest friend—and no one gives it a thought ! For the first few days that follow death people do think of it, because such is the custom, or perhaps even for the space of a year ; and after that, the persons to whom you manifested so much affection are left to burn unaided. Oh, how truly do they then estimate the value of your love ! and how great a folly it is to rely on the friendship of creatures, and how good it is to attach one's self to God only, who is the true friend in life, in death, and after death ! There are well-authenticated revelations from which we learn that there are souls which are condemned to the fires of Purgatory for hundreds of years, and sometimes, alas ! for the indulgence of some vanity—a woman perhaps for her love of dress : and, knowing all this, you forget them so soon and so easily.

I said in my book on "The Admirable Mother of God," how profitable a thing it is to place all our good works in her sacred hands, that she may apply them to such souls as she pleases : do you at least place at her disposal the good works of some months or years of your life ; perhaps, for what you know, all that is wanting to deliver a soul from Purgatory is some one single good action. Father de Coret, of the Company of Jesus, in his work on "Devotion to the Holy Angel Guardians," relates two very striking incidents bearing on this subject. He says that a soul suffering in Purgatory learned from his good angel that a child just born would one day be a priest, and would deliver him from that place of suffering by his first offering of the Holy Sacrifice. He adds, what I have already related, that in the year 1634, in the city of Vienna, three other souls appeared to a Jesuit, and told him that at his birth their good angels had brought them the news in the flames of Purgatory, assuring them that one day he should be their deliverer. St Teresa has written that she had a revelation that the soul of one of her benefactors was to come out of Purgatory on the day that the first Mass should be celebrated in one of her houses ; and this made her feel very anxious to hasten on the completion of that house, knowing that this soul would continue to burn until the Holy Sacrifice of the Mass could be celebrated within its walls. I leave you to make such reflections as these revelations may suggest, if only your mind be a little enlightened; they will furnish many and most profitable thoughts.

ELEVENTH PRACTICE
To Practise some Virtue, or abstain from some Vice, nr honour of the Holy Angels.

If we desire truly to love the angels, we must love what they love and hate what they hate. This being so, we must have a love for virtue and an aversion for vice. They require of us (says a holy Father) sobriety, chastity, voluntary poverty, frequent aspirations Heavenward, and, above all, truth and peace. That young nobleman, Falcone, was well persuaded of the truth of these maxims : he had promised, in honour of his good angel, always to speak the truth, and having killed a man, he frankly avowed his guilt, to avoid telling a lie, although there had been no witness of the deed ; choosing rather to lose his life than break his promise to his good angel. Behold him, then, led forth to death : but as the executioner was raising his arm to cut off his head, an angel appeared and prevented him ; arresting also the arms of three others who came forward to strike the fatal blow. This miracle obtained his pardon ; and he afterwards changed his name from Falcone to that of Angelo, and quitted the world, henceforward to converse only with angels.

Humility, purity, and prayer are the sweet virtues which these heavenly spirits look for in those who make profession of honouring them. They cannot endure the proud, and humility is their prime virtue, which, indeed, they are themselves continually exercising amongst us.

Purity is absolutely necessary in order to be admitted to their friendship ; they are the friends of the chaste, and specially of virgins ; for the purer men are (says St Ambrose) the dearer are they to the angels

: hence virginity is called an angelic virtue, and they who practise it are styled angels upon earth ; and justly so, since it is they who bear the closest resemblance to these pure spirits. O ye virgins, whoever ye be, remember that you possess a treasure of inestimable value, and one which is to be preferred before crowns and empires : if its worth were known, our earth would become a heaven, and every one would feel a holy passion for it It was the virtue dear to Jesus, Mary, and Joseph ; to St John the Baptist, the precursor of Jesus; to St John the Evangelist, His beloved disciple; and the great Apostle protests (1 Cor. vii 7) through the light that was given him, that he would that all the world practised it. It is our Master's great counsel of perfection, and its privileges are inexpressible, and shall endure throughout eternity. No life is too precious to be lost for its preservation, no pain but ought to be endured, no pleasure but ought to be renounced. And here I cannot refrain from a passing observation concerning the wonder I feel at seeing many directors forward in recommending marriage to persons who have an attraction for this virtue, under the pretext of certain difficulties which may stand in the way. Truly, truly, everything ought to be done to preserve so precious a grace. No, never will the Adorable Jesus be wanting to such as, in order to please Him the more, pass their lives in celibacy. He is the same God who has assisted so many virgins, and at so tender an age ; who has fortified their courage ; who has sustained them against all the rage of devils and of men. O men of little faith that we are ! a fly can terrify us, the least difficulty damps our courage, while all that is needed is but to make one good resolution. God can give none but good counsels; and we cannot do better than generously follow them.

Prayer is the other virtue which renders us most like to the angels : accordingly we have seen them assisting in a wonderful manner such persons as have addicted themselves to its exercise. St Bernard had one day the consolation of seeing them chronicling the prayers of his religious, some in letters of gold, others in letters of silver, while some they marked with ink, and some with water, according to the fervour and tepidity of their interior dispositions.

These heavenly spirits are painted barefooted and treading on clouds, to signify to us their complete disengagement from all earthly things. They breathe only God alone, and they feel a holy jealousy for the least things which concern His Divine interests. St Jerome relates, in reference to this, a very terrible story, which sufficiently shows how jealous the angels are for the interests of their Sovereign. Hymetius, the husband of Pretextata, and uncle of the virgin Eustochium, had desired his wife to deck out this virgin in gay apparel, and make her fair in the eyes of men, hoping by this means to divert her from her love of virginity. But no sooner had this woman complied with her husband's wishes, than the angel of the Lord, full of holy indignation, appeared to her, and spoke to her these words, which the Father of the Church whom I have quoted records:—"You have dared, then, to prefer a husband's commands to those of Jesus Christ, and have had the presumption to touch the head of a virgin with your sacrilegious hands? Those hands shall now become withered, that by this punishment you may be made to feel what it is you have done ; and in five months' time you shall be led into the road to hell; and if you persevere in your crime you shall lose at once both your husband and your children." Now this great Doctor of the Church affirms that all came to pass as the angel had foretold.

If, then, you wish to be devout to the holy angels, you must endeavour to please them; and to please them you must persevere in the solid practice of virtue. Study particularly, with God's assistance, to acquire such virtues as are most dear to them, and most necessary to yourself ; and at the same time use every possible endeavour to extirpate in yourself all that may be displeasing to them. Wage, then, a perpetual war against sin, and, above all, against impurity. St Basil said that this sin drives away the holy angels from us, as smoke drives away bees, and a putrid smell, doves. It is related of this saint that, being habitually favoured with a heavenly vision before celebrating the Holy Mysteries, and being one day deprived of it, he learned that it was owing to the presence of a deacon, who had fallen into impurity ; and, on causing him to withdraw, he immediately enjoyed his usual privilege. The angel of St Frances, that devout client of these amiable favourites of Jesus and Mary, whom she always beheld under a visible form, used to hide his eyes whenever the least fault or imperfection was committed in his presence. Have a care, then, not to do anything which may offend eyes which are constantly beholding you ; and, as we have all some predominant passion, some inclination which cleaves to us more particularly, and which is the source of almost all our disorders, set yourself to combat this disposition in honour of the holy angels ; make it from time to time the subject of your particular examinations of conscience, and observe whether you are correcting yourself of it ; undertake to offer every day to your holy angel some mortification of this taste or inclination : it is the most acceptable present you can make him ; and remember that it is no legitimate excuse to say that this is our weak point ; those who are in hell have gone there through that very inclination, which they did not subdue, through that weakness, which has worked their ruin. It is by their weak point that the devil ensnares men, and catches souls; it is there that we ought to be most upon our guard, and have the greatest need of angelic protection.

St Bernard advises us often to call to mind the presence of our Guardian Angel, in order to keep us from falling into our usual faults. This is a very profitable thought, and is a great help to us in overcoming them. It is a remarkable thing that even ancient philosophers have given this counsel. One of these philosophers relates that this was Plato's opinion, as I have read in the book entitled "The Angel-Guardian" of Father Drexelius, where this philosopher is quoted as having said that all men have invisible witnesses who are ever present with them, and who observe, not their actions only, but also their thoughts ; and that, after the death of each, the witness who has watched over him conducts him to receive the judgment which is passed upon his life, according to the testimony he renders of it : wherefore, continues this author, all ye who, in listening to me, hear the divine sentiment of Plato, so dispose all your actions and all your thoughts as men who must know that they have nothing hidden from these witnesses or guardians, whether internally or externally. He then goes on to speak of the protection which this witness renders, who, he declares ought to be religiously honoured and recognised, as he was by Socrates, by the innocence and justice of his life. Would you not say that it was a Christian who was here speaking ? and. would any one believe that these were the thoughts and sentiments of a Pagan ?

TWELFTH PRACTICE.
To Promote in all kinds of Ways Devotion to the Nine Choirs of Holy Angels.

If the holy angels do all that can be done for the service of men, men on their part are bound not to spare themselves, but to make use of all possible means, within the order of God, for the augmentation of their glory ; and since not only the angels of the lowest choir, but the angels of all the hierarchies, lovingly watch over us, our gratitude to them ought to be as comprehensive as our duties towards them ; and since God only is the one great and urgent motive which ought to prompt our actions, and since this motive reigns supreme in all the choirs of angels, but in a more special manner in the highest, who have most loved our most amiable God, and have been most loved by Him, this alone ought to be sufficient to make us have a singular devotion to them all, and endeavour to promote that devotion in others in every possible way. A good heart will enter readily into these sentiments : we have only to love to be persuaded of their justice, and to make firm resolutions to labour with all our power to promote the glory of the angels.

If you should still ask me what you ought to do, I reply that I have said everything in saying that yon ought to omit nothing, but do everything, and labour with all your might, within the order of God, to promote devotion to the holy angels. Reflect on these few words, and you will perceive that they furnish you with ample matter ; and that if you understand them well and practise them, we may then believe that your love for the angels is truly sincere : the great thing is to have a real love for these amiable beings ; for if it be real, I need only quote to you that beautiful saying of St Augustine, "Love, and then do what you please." Love is full of devices and fertile in inventions ; it will suggest to you abundance of ways whereby to increase the honour paid to these princes of Heaven, for such is the nature of cordial and genuine love.

However, to tell you simply my own notions, it appears to me that one of the means which may serve to make them more honoured, is to distribute pictures of these glorious spirits, particularly to the poor people in country places, and, indeed, also to the poor in towns, among whom there is greater ignorance than is generally supposed ; experience proving that numbers of persons even in the largest cities have but little knowledge of the mysteries of our holy religion. We may suggest to the rich and to our personal friends the keeping of such pictures in their rooms; the sight of them carries on the mind to the objects represented, and often sensibly touches the heart. St Chrysostom, on seeing a picture of the holy angel who discomfited the army of Sennacherib, was melted by it even to tears. If we have the means of presenting pictures to be placed in churches, or in some chapel, or over some altar, it is an excellent way of exciting devotion to them among the people. Constantine the Great caused four images of the holy angels to be made ; they were of an extraordinary size, and all resplendent with the brilliancy of the precious stones with which they were richly adorned.

Another excellent means, and one of the best, as it appears to me, is to make a large distribution of well-selected books composed on the subject, or take occasion to invite persons to purchase some. I know of nothing better calculated to promote their honour. This means includes almost all the others, since it both gives them honour and teaches it. Amongst many books of this kind, the "Clock of the Guardian Angel," by Father Drexelius; "Devotion to the Angels," by Father de Bary; "Devotion to the Angels," by Father Nouet ; "Devotion to the Holy Angel-Guardians," by Father de Coret, all four Religious of the Company of Jesus, recommend love and devotion to these blessed spirits with so much sweetness and persuasiveness, that I think it would be difficult to read them without being sensibly affected, and without conceiving a lively desire to honour them greatly for the remainder of one's life.

Such as are rich will contribute much to the glory of the angels by employing their wealth in erecting a church or chapel or an altar in honour of them, and so much the more as by this means they will work for the glory of the holy angels, not only during their lifetime, but as long as these buildings shall last ; which will be the means of drawing all manner of persons to honour them, many of whom would otherwise never have thought of it. Such was the devotion of the Emperor Constantine, who raised two magnificent temples in honour of St Michael. The Emperor Justinian erected six in honour of that archangel and the other angels. St Helena had another built in honour of these Intelligences, on the spot where the angel is believed to have appeared to the shepherds. Persons whose means are not equal to such an outlay, can at least present ornaments for their chapels, have lights burned in them, and give pictures to them. I have noticed in another place that the Sovereign Pontiff Julius III. dedicated a church in honour of the seven highest princes who stand before the throne of God.

Zealous preachers will do much towards establishing devotion to the angels, if they will instruct the people in it, and from time to time powerfully exhort them to it. I know some who would be very sorry to leave any place where they had been preaching without a sermon on the subject of these glorious spirits ; and the effects which result from this show that it is one of the most profitable means that can be employed. It rests with those priests whom God calls to preach in different towns and provinces to make good use of this means ; and I have no doubt but that if such were the practice, we should in a short time have the consolation of seeing devotion to the holy angels established everywhere. What is to hinder a preacher, when giving his Advent or Lent sermons, from allotting a day or two to discourses in their honour? Missionaries in the course of their missions might easily do the same, with the addition of a few catechetical instructions to make souls acquainted with the angelic perfections and goodness. Seculars may found such sermons and catechisms in churches, endowing them with revenue for that purpose.

The master of a family in his house, a father among his children, a person living in the country among the peasants, or when visiting the poor or bestowing alms upon them, may promote this devotion by teaching what ought to be believed concerning the angels, and telling them of the assistance men receive from them; recommending practices with which they can be honoured, and making those over whom they have authority perform them ; relating at the same time some examples calculated to dispose and attract persons to this devotion. We may do the same with those in whose company we are travelling, taking occasion from the multitude of angels in the different places through which we pass, even saluting them publicly and in the presence of others, so as to furnish an opportunity of conversing about them

Archdeacons, and other visitors of parochial churches, can exhort the priests of these churches to give every year exhortations or catechetical instructions on this devotion. This also is one of the best means that can be adopted for spreading it everywhere. The visitors of regulars can also contribute much towards it in the monasteries and convents under their jurisdiction ; all superiors in the houses dependent on them; but, above all, prelates in their dioceses, by establishing associations in honour of these exalted spirits in various places, taking occasion from time to time to recommend pastors and preachers during Advent and Lent to make the people acquainted with these confraternities, and thus showing the interest they take in the matter, and proving how agreeable it would be to them that this devotion should be encouraged.

In fine, zealous persons may meet and confer together about the means of establishing and augmenting this devotion ; they can speak to the prelates to whom they can gain access, to priests and superiors ; they can write letters to different parts of the country where they have connexions, and cultivate holy acquaintances there for this end, send books, and procure the foundation of some pious association.

Conclusion of this Little Work, by the Plan of an Association in Honour of the Nine Choirs of Angels.

There are many confraternities or associations, instituted for various purposes—though God Himself is always the first and primary object, as is absolutely necessary. Some have for their end deliverance from some temporal evil : thus we see confraternities in honour of St Sebastian for preservation from plague, and others in honour of St Firmin for relief from the gout Others again regard only spiritual interests ; as, for example, to obtain the grace of a good death and to be saved from hell. Now that of which I am here speaking would have but one and a very simple end in everything, the sole interest of God only, in an entire forgetfulness of all that is not God; and as His interests are concerned in the establishment of the empire of Jesus and Mary throughout the earth, it would have for its end the happy reign of this Adorable King and this great Queen of angels and of men. There are such multitudes in all the earth who are occupied with their own interests and with the interests of their fellow-creatures ; it is self-interest which gives the impulse to everything and sets everything in motion, which causes division between nearest relatives, and is the source of all disputes and all law-suits, of sadness, and weariness, and disquietude, of wars between States, of eagerness in all transactions, of disturbance in all consciences, in fine, of all the miseries we see in this wretched life. If some are to be met with who are disengaged from temporal interests, you will detect imperfection in their attachment to their spiritual interests ; in short, it is very rare to meet with souls who no longer desire anything but God only. It would be the object of this devotion to provide a remedy for this, by looking only to the pure interests of God. Alas ! the streets of towns are full of a crowd of people, their palaces are thronged with multitudes passing in and out, hurrying to and fro, and disquieting themselves in the pursuit of their own interests. People post about, undertake long and arduous journeys, cross the seas, expose themselves to death a thousand times, run to the very extremities of the earth, abandon relatives, children, friends, and all that is sweetest in life to forward these interests; armies are levied, soldiers mustered, life sacrificed in their defence. People engage themselves in states of life for which they have no vocation, thus risking their eternal salvation for the sake of upholding their honour, enjoying the revenues of benefices, obtaining some office; and they compromise the salvation of their children in like manner. It is the great God of Eternity whose interests are alone neglected. Alas! what do men do for this sacred cause ? Now the object of this association is to bind souls together for so noble an end, and to form holy troops for the great King Jesus and His amiable Mother, whom He has associated with His glory and called to share His crowns.

The association would be in honour of all the nine choirs of angels, to beg them to join with us, and make a holy union of heaven and earth, in order to obtain the advent of the kingdom of God. As these spirits are perfectly disinterested, and have never had the slightest movement of self-interest, having always been lost in an abyss of pure love, the love of God only, fighting from the very beginning of the world for the interests of God, and in the cause of the Incarnate Word, we cannot choose better protectors or more powerful intercessors to hasten the blessed reign of the pure love of Jesus and Mary. We honour them all, we invoke them all, that we may call all Heaven to our aid, and make our union stronger against the rage of hell and the malice of men, who labour unceasingly to destroy the empire of God by the empire of sin.

The associates on the day of their admission, or some days previous, will make a general confession of their whole life, if they have never made one before, taking care, in case they have already made one, not to repeat it through scrupulosity ; they will therefore do nothing in this matter but by the advice of their director. These confessions are very necessary in country districts, many of the poor people being ashamed of confessing their sins to priests whom they are constantly seeing. This is why it is well that their pastors should volunteer to suggest their availing themselves of some good extraordinary confessor, having regard, not only to his capacity and kindness, but to their own willingness and readiness to open their hearts to him, giving them to understand that they would themselves be glad to see them profit by this opportunity, and, far from looking coldly on their doing so, or testifying any repugnance, inviting them to it gently and repeatedly. Besides the shame which persons experience at confessing mortal sins, the want of compunction and of the purpose of amendment makes a good general confession, with a review of their whole life, a matter of necessity.

The members will go to communion on the day of admission, and annually on the feast of St Michael, as well as on the first day or the first Sunday in March ; and they should be exhorted to do so also every month, on the Sunday selected for specially honouring the holy angels.

Every day they will recite nine times the *Gloria Patri*, or the Angelical Salutation, in honour of the nine choirs of holy angels, and from time to time remember to repeat these words, as an ejaculatory prayer : "*Pater, adveniat regnum Tuum*—Father, Thy kingdom come;" but these words they ought to utter far more with the heart than with the lips, conceiving ardent desires for the reign of Jesus and Mary.

The most convenient Sunday in the month might be chosen, and the one least taken up with the devotions of other confraternities, as, for instance, the third ; and on that day, after the manner of the other pious confraternities, a Mass might be celebrated in honour of the angels, if that can conveniently be done, and if there be several priests in the parish, as the Sunday office must not be interfered with If there be but one priest, who is obliged to say the parish Mass, there might be a procession after Vespers, hymns and responses being sung in honour of these glorious spirits, and the image of a holy angel, designed for the purpose, might be borne on the occasion ; if possible, there should also be a sermon, or some short discourse or instruction on the subject of this devotion.

Every year a day might be specially set apart as the great feast of the association, for instance, St Michael's day, at the end of September; or, seeing that the dwellers in towns are often in the country at that time, and the country people are still occupied with finishing their harvest or vintage, the first Sunday in March might be taken, which would make it easy to procure a preacher, as being the season of Lent ; or the first Sunday after the eighth of May, when the feast of the Apparition of St Michael is kept, and on this day the Ordinary's permission might be asked for having the Blessed Sacrament exposed; It might be carried in procession, and solemn Mass said; a sermon might be preached; and all the associates should not fail to communicate on that day and to celebrate it with all possible devotion. On the vigil, if the members are not disposed to fast, unless it be within the season of Lent, they might at least observe some abstinence; and, as a preparation for the feast, they might visit some poor person, or bestow some alms, if their means allowed. They might also visit some chapel, or altar, dedicated to God under the invocation of these princes of Heaven.

Every Tuesday should be a day of peculiar devotion, specially consecrated to these blessed spirits. The members should hear Mass on that day in their honour, where they have the facility of so doing, and should remember to make a more than usually attentive meditation upon them. The feast of our Lady of Angels, which is celebrated on the second of August, ought to be held in especial veneration, as the day on which the Ever-Blessed Virgin is honoured in the character of their Sovereign and beloved Lady and Mistress.

There should be a register or book in which to inscribe the names of all the associates of both sexes, who should be received by the superior of the association, or by some one deputed on his part, no money being taken on admission, that the poorest may have every facility for joining the Confraternity, each person being free to give, according to his or her devotion, towards decorating the altar and providing lights and other requisites. I have no doubt but that in large towns sufficient money would always be contributed for having Masses said and meeting other necessary expenses; but as there might be more difficulty in villages, endeavours ought to be made to obtain some endowment, which, indeed, would also be desirable in towns; and some small trifle might be received, say two sous yearly, from each member, care, however, being taken to ask nothing of the poor ; and to this end there should be a treasurer, who would receive what was contributed, and give in his or her account each year, on a day fixed by the Confraternity.

Every three months, or, at least, twice a year, the superior with the principal members of the association should assemble to deliberate upon the means of establishing and augmenting devotion to the holy angels ; and for this purpose the preceding chapter might be read, which suggests different methods, and each might propose with simplicity his own lights on the subject.

All the members ought to recollect that the end of the association being the reign of Jesus and Mary, which can be established only through the knowledge and love of God, they are under a special obligation to have their children and servants instructed in the mysteries of the faith, and themselves to learn its most necessary truths, of which they are too often ignorant. They should not fail to teach them to the poor whom they assist, or to whom they give alms ; to use all the influence in their power with bishops and pastors to have the catechism carefully taught ; to procure also, according to their ability, the sending of missions into country places ; and, above all, to contribute all they can towards foreign missions, which are the means of establishing the kingdom of Jesus Christ in those pagan countries which are subject to the tyranny of the devil.

They ought also to bestow great care on the Blessed Sacrament of the Altar, and all that is connected with It : as ciboriums, chalices, tabernacles, decorations, corporals, altars ; and they should endeavour to accompany It when carried to the sick, preserving also great modesty of demeanour in the churches, having a horror of the least irreverences committed there, never talking in them, and labouring to put a stop to the immodest behaviour of others. They should be exhorted to frequent the sacraments with the proper dispositions, to practise mental prayer, to read spiritual books, to examine their conscience regularly, to offer their prayers to God together with their families every evening, to assist the poor, and to give themselves to the solid practice of all other virtues.

They must fly with horror both sin and all the occasions of sin, above all, impurity, which is the sin most opposed to the purity of the angels. They must avoid everything which leads to it; as too great intimacy between persons of different sexes, words with a double meaning, unbecoming familiarities, songs or books in any degree calculated to shock chaste ears, and labour for the destruction of this accursed sin, the great enemy of the reign of Jesus Christ, not only in their own persons, but in all to whom they may have access. They should strive to gain to our Lord such souls as are unhappily entangled in this vice, and with a sweet and cordial charity provide them with the necessary means of living, in order to draw them from it, taking care not to give occasion to their continuing in sin, either by failing to render them assistance, or by any contemptuous repulse and a certain hardness of heart, for which many shall have to render strict account at the dread tribunal of God. All enmities, disputes, slanders ought to be banished from the hearts of those who profess to love the angels; nay, they ought to love those who hate them, and do good to those who injure them.

Finally, in large towns, nine days might be appropriated to honouring the nine choirs of angels with great solemnity. Daring that period the Blessed Sacrament might be exposed, with the exception of the times when people are assembled to hear the sermon (and this is a point worthy of much attention, for a thousand irreverences are committed on such occasions) : if possible, there should be a sermon every day, and the office of the angels should be said upon days when nothing else interferes ; each day there should be High Mass, and Benediction in the evening, and nothing should be omitted which is customary on the greatest festivals, or which devout piety can suggest For this purpose, some time ought to be chosen as free as may be from other feasts, that there may be more opportunity for saying the office of the angels. It would seem that *Quasimodo* (Low) Sunday might be very suitable for commencing this solemnity, as it often occurs in the month of April, which is not much occupied with feasts ; besides which, it is at that time that the towns are fullest, so that a greater concourse of persons might be expected.

A PRAYER TO THE NINE CHOIRS OF HOLY ANGELS.

Blessed spirits of the heavenly court, invincible champions of the cause of God, after having adored, praised, blessed, and given thanks to the God of all goodness, for the incomparable graces with which He has enriched you; after having made a sincere protestation with our whole heart, that we take all possible interest therein, rejoicing because of the joy and ineffable glory which you possess ; after having besought you benignantly to accept the inviolable resolution we now take to have a special devotion to you for the remainder of our days, and to promote its establishment and increase by every means in our power wherever we can, we implore the aid of all your glorious bands, for the advancement of the reign of the Adorable Jesus and the amiable Mary over all heathens, heretics, schismatics, over all persons who live in true submission to the Holy, Catholic, Apostolic, and Roman Church, and particularly over the Sovereign Pontiff, who is its one visible head on earth, and over all other prelates ; so that, all people professing the same faith, cleaving to the purity of its maxims, and leading a life conformable to its rules, the sacred interests of God Only may live and reign in all hearts throughout all ages. This is the grace for which we ask, O mighty princes of the heavenly host, from the Father of Mercies, through your powerful intercession ; this is the consolation which we beseech the God of all consolation to grant us ; that His Name may be sanctified, His Kingdom come, His Will be done on earth as it is in heaven ; that the empire of sin and of the devils may be destroyed ; that the Gospel may be preached to all nations, and received throughout all the earth ; that the Holy Name of God may be honoured and glorified ; that all spirits may bless the Lord, adore Him, love Him, and live in perfect and entire submission to His Divine Will. Come, then, O ye Angels and Archangels, hasten to establish the dominion of God in kingdoms and provinces, in towns and country-places, and in all who dwell therein ; ye sacred Principalities, rule all hearts, possess them, that you may subject them to the empire of Jesus and Mary ; ye admirable Powers, confound the devils, who oppose themselves thereto, defeat the designs of hell, and the malice of all sorcerers and magicians, and other enemies of God ; ye divine Virtues, lead souls to walk in the solid paths of Divine love ; ye glorious Dominations, make known to men, to this end, the will of God concerning them ; ye amiable Thrones, establish in their inmost hearts that peace which our Lord bequeathed to us ; ye Cherubim, princes of heavenly science, communicate its excellent light to our earth ; and ye Seraphim, princes of pure love, cause men to live only by its flames, that God Only may be the true Sovereign and the absolute Master of all we are, and all we do. Amen. Amen. Amen. God Only, God Only, God Only.

POSTSCRIPT.

God, who commanded the light to shine out of darkness, and who calls things that are not as things that are, having been pleased to extract His own glory from my abjection and nothingness, has poured so abundant a benediction upon the little work of Devotion to the Nine Choirs of Holy Angels, which His Divine Providence, ever my good and most faithful mother, has made me present to the public, that it has been translated into foreign languages, and an ex-provincial of the Religious of the Company of Jesus in Poland, who had already translated it into Polish, has even bound himself by vow to translate it also into Latin. Thus, it is, according to what the Apostle says to the Corinthians (1 Cor. i. 27-29), that God chooses those who seem to be fools in the world to confound the wise, and the weak to confound the strong, and that He makes use of such as are vile and contemptible, yea, and of nothingness itself, that no man may glory in His sight.

Having spoken of the profanations which take place with respect to the Sacred Body of our Lord, we think we ought to suggest that one great means of preventing many which occur from particles becoming detached and so falling to the ground, when communion is being given to the people, would be to fasten the lid to the ciborium, and hold it under the mouth of those who communicate, that it may receive any such particles : this is why the deacon carries the paten at High Mass, and places it under the mouth of the communicants.

LITANY OF THE HOLY ANGELS.

Lord, have mercy.
Lord, have mercy.
Christ, have mercy.
Christ, have mercy.
Lord, have mercy.
Lard, have mercy.
Christ, hear us.
Christ, graciously hear us.

Have, &c.

God the Father of heaven,
God the Son, Redeemer of the world,
God the Holy Ghost,
Holy Trinity, one God,
Holy Mary, Queen of Angels,
Holy Mother of God,
Holy Virgin of virgins,
St Michael, who wast ever the defender of the people of God,

Pray for us.

St Michael, who didst drive from heaven Lucifer and his rebel crew,
St Michael, who didst cast down to hell the accuser of our brethren,
St Gabriel, who didst expound to Daniel the heavenly vision,

St Gabriel, who didst foretell to Zachary the birth and ministry of John the Baptist,
St Gabriel, who didst announce to Mary the Incarnation of the Divine Word,
St Raphael, who didst lead Tobias safe through his journey to his home again,
St Raphael, who didst deliver Sara from the devil,
St Raphael, who didst restore his sight to Tobias the elder,
All ye holy Angels, who stand upon the high and lofty throne of God,
Who cry to Him continually, Holy, holy, holy,
Who dispel the darkness of our minds, and give us light,
Who are the messengers of heavenly things to men,
Who have been appointed by God to be our guardians,
Who always behold the face of our Father who is in heaven,
Who rejoice over one sinner doing penance,
Who struck the Sodomites with blindness,
Who led Loth out of the midst of the ungodly,
Who ascended and descended on the ladder of Jacob,
Who delivered the divine law to Moses on mount Sinai,
Who brought good tidings when Christ was born, Who ministered to Him in the desert,
Who comforted Him in His agony,
Who sat in white garments at His sepulchre,
Who appeared to the disciples as He went up into heaven,
Who shall go before Him bearing the standard of the Cross, when He cometh to judgment,
Who shall gather together the elect at the end of the world,
Who shall separate the wicked from among the just,
Who offer to God the prayers of them that pray,
Who assist us at the hour of death,
Who carried Lazarus into Abraham's bosom,
Who conduct to heaven the souls of the just, cleansed from every stain,
Who perform signs and wonders by the power of God,

Who are sent to minister for those who shall receive the inheritance of salvation,
Who would cure Babylon, and when she will not be cured, depart and forsake her,
Who are set over kingdoms and provinces,
Who have often put to flight armies of enemies,
Who have often delivered God's servants from prison, and other perils of this life,
Who have often consoled the holy martyrs in their torments,
Who are wont to cherish with peculiar care the prelates and princes of the Church, and all that are under their charge,
All ye holy orders of blessed Spirits,
From all dangers,

Deliver us &c.

Deliver us, O Lord, by Thy holy Angels.
From the snares of the devil,
From All heresy and schism,
From plague, famine, and war,
From sudden and unlooked for death,
From everlasting death,
We sinners,
Beseech Thee, hear us.
Through Thy holy Angels,
That Thou wouldst spare us,
That Thou wouldst pardon us,
That Thou wouldst vouchsafe to govern and preserve Thy holy Church,

We beseech thee hear us.

That Thou wouldst vouchsafe to protect our Apostolic Prelate, and all ecclesiastical orders,

That Thou wouldst vouchsafe to grant peace and security to kings and all Christian princes,

That Thou wouldst vouchsafe to give and preserve the fruits of the earth,

That Thou wouldst vouchsafe to grant eternal rest to all the faithful departed,

Lamb of God, who takest away the sins of the world,

Spare us, O Lord.

Lamb of God, who takest away the sins of the world,

Graciously hear us, O Lord.

Lamb of God, who takest away the sins of the world,

Have mercy on us.

Lord, have mercy.

Christ, have mercy.

Lord, have mercy.

> Our Father, &c. (secretly).
>
> v. Bless the Lord, all ye His Angels.
>
> R. Ye that are mighty in strength, that fulfil His commandments, hearkening unto the voice of His words.
>
> v. Bless the Lord, all ye His hosts.
>
> R. Ye ministers of His, that do His will.
>
> v. He hath given His Angels charge concerning thee.
>
> R. To keep thee in all thy ways.
>
> v. The Angel of the Lord shall encamp round about them that fear Him.
>
> R. And shall deliver them.
>
> v. In the sight of the Angels will I sing unto Thee, O my God.
>
> R. I will worship toward Thy holy temple, and will give praise unto Thy Name, O Lord.
>
> v. O Lord, hear my prayer.
>
> R. And let my cry come unto Thee.

Let us pray.

O God, who dispensest the services of angels and men in a wonderful order, mercifully grant that our life may be protected on earth by those who always do Thee service in heaven. Through Jesus Christ our Lord. Amen.

A PRAYER TO ALL ANGELS.

Ye Angels, so holy and so pure, spirits truly blessed, who stand before your Lord, and contemplate with such exceeding joy the Divine Countenance of that Heavenly Solomon, who hath enlightened you with a wisdom so excellent, who hath ennobled you with so many prerogatives, and hath made you worthy of so eminent a glory—you, I say, who are those brilliant stars which shine with so much lustre in the empyreal Heaven, pour into my soul, I beseech you, your blessed influences, preserve my faith in its purity, my hope in its firmness, my virtue in its integrity, and make me to advance ever in the love of God and of my neighbour. I beseech you also, O ye blessed Angels, that you will be pleased by your heavenly guidance, to lead me along the path of humility, of which you gave us the example in your own blessed beginnings, that after this life I may merit with you to contemplate the sovereign beauty of the Heavenly Father, and to occupy the place of some one of those stars which through their pride have fallen from Heaven.

LITANY OF OUR HOLY ANGEL-GUARDIAN.

Have, &c.

Lord, have mercy.
Lord, have mercy.
Christ, have mercy.
Christy have mercy.
Lord, have mercy.
Lord, have mercy.
Christ, hear us.
Christ, graciously hear us.
God the Father of heaven,
God the Son, Redeemer of the world,
God the Holy Ghost,
Holy Trinity, one God,
Holy Mary, Queen of Angels,

Pray for us.

Holy Angel, my guardian,
Holy Angel, my prince,
Holy Angel, my monitor,
Holy Angel, my counsellor,
Holy Angel, my defender,
Holy Angel, my steward,
Holy Angel, my friend,
Holy Angel, my negotiator,

Holy Angel, my intercessor,
Holy Angel, my patron,
Holy Angel, my director,
Holy Angel, my ruler,
Holy Angel, my protector,
Holy Angel, my comforter,
Holy Angel, my brother,
Holy Angel, my teacher,
Holy Angel, my shepherd,
Holy Angel, my witness,
Holy Angel, my helper,
Holy Angel, my watcher,
Holy Angel, my conductor,
Holy Angel, my preserver,
Holy Angel, my instructor,
Holy Angel, my enlightener,
Lamb of God, who takest away the sins of the world,
Spare us, O Lord.
Lamb of God, who takest away the sins of the world,
Graciously hear us, O Lord.
Lamb of God, who takest away the sins of the world,
Have mercy on us.
Christ, hear us.
Christ, graciously hear us.

   v. Pray for us, 0 holy Angel-Guardian,
   R. That we may be made worthy of the promises of Christ.

Let us pray.

Almighty, everlasting God, who, in the counsel of Thy ineffable goodness, hast appointed to all the faithful, from their mother's womb, a special Angel-Guardian of their body and soul ; grant that I may so love and honour him whom Thou hast so mercifully given me, that, protected by the bounty of Thy grace, and by his assistance, I may merit to behold, with him and all the angelic host, the glory of Thy countenance in the heavenly country. Who livest and reignest, world without end. Amen.

A PRAYER TO OUR ANGEL-GUARDIAN.

O most faithful companion, whom God hast appointed to watch over me, my guide and protector, ever at my side, what thanks can I offer thee for thy love, thy constancy, and thy innumerable benefits ? Thou watchest over me in sleep, thou consolest me in sorrow, thou raisest me when I fall, thou wardest off dangers, thou preparest me for the future, thou withdrawest me from sin, thou urgest me to good, thou movest me to do penance, and reconcilest me with my God. Already, perhaps, I should have been thrust into hell, unless thou by thy prayers hadst averted from me the dreadful wrath of God. Desert me not, then, I beseech thee ; encourage me in adversity, restrain me in prosperity, protect me in dangers, and assist me in temptations, lest at any time I yield to them. Offer to the Divine Majesty all my prayers and sighs and works, and obtain for me the grace to die in the friendship of God, and so to enter into life eternal. Amen.

TRANSLATOR'S NOTES.

Note A. Page 28.

This remarkable story figures as an "example" in several pious books; we find it, for instance, in F. Nieremberg's "Treatise on the Temporal and Eternal," where it is related as follows :—"Johannes Major, or John of Tours, reports (Ex. 14) that a certain monk being at matins, with the other religious of his monastery, and coming to that verse of Psalm lxxix., where it is said, A thousand years in the presence of God are but as yesterday, which is already past, began to imagine with himself how it might be possible ; and remaining in choir (as his manner was) after the end of matins, to finish his devotions, he humbly besought the Lord to grant him the true understanding of that place ; which he had no sooner done but he perceived a little bird in the choir, that, with flying up and down before him, by little and little, with her melodious singing, insensibly drew him out of the church into a wood not far off, where, perching herself upon a hough, she for some short time, as it seemed to him, continued her music, to the unspeakable delight of the monk, and then flew away, leaving him by her absence no less sad and pensive. But, seeing she came no more, he returned back, thinking he had left his monastery the same morning, immediately after matins, and that it was now about the third hour ; but, coming to the convent, which was near the wood, he found the gate by which he was accustomed to enter to be closed up, and another opened in some other part, where, calling upon the porter, he was asked who he was, from whence he came, and what was his business. He answered that he was the sacristan of the church, and that, having that morning gone abroad after matins, he found all things at his return changed. The porter demanded of him the name of the abbot, the prior, the procurator. He named them all, and wondered he was neither understood nor permitted to enter, and when they feigned not to know those religious whom he mentioned, desired to be brought to the abbot; but coming into his presence, neither the abbot knew him, nor he the abbot, whereat the good monk, being much astonished, knew not what to say. The abbot asked him his name, and that of his abbot; and, turning over the annals of the monastery, found it was more than three hundred years since the death of those persons whom he named. Whereupon the monk, making a relation of what had happened to him concerning the psalm, they acknowledged him, and admitted him as a brother into their profession, where, having received the sacraments of the Church, he with much peace ended his days in our Lord."—B. iv. c. 1.

The legend is related at greater length in the "Prato Fiorito" of F. Valerio (a Capuchin), who cites it from a book which he calls "Speculum Exemplorum," by one Henrico. The translator has been unable to trace the story to its origin; neither has he succeeded in finding the passage in Cornelius à Lapide to which Boudon refers. Such stories are of frequent occurrence in books of piety, and are usually intended merely as illustrations of some practical lesson or spiritual truth, just as many popular anecdotes are introduced into works of secular or moral instruction, without the retailer of them intending thereby to represent them as possessed of any historical value, much less to vouch for their circumstantial accuracy. But in this instance Cornelius à Lapide is said to have examined carefully into the evidence for the legend, and to have convinced himself that it was of a substantial character. If this be so, and the story be really authentic, we may find some sort of analogy for it in the ancient and generally received tradition of the Church, that Enoch and Elias are miraculously reserved by God to re-appear in the last times as the "Two Witnesses" of whom St John prophesies (Apoc. xi. 3). And, if so reserved, what more probable than that their supernaturally prolonged life is one perpetual ecstasy? The reader may not be sorry to be reminded of a beautiful legend which the Countess Hahn-Hahn mentions in her "Lives of the Fathers of the Desert" (Pp. 45, 46) as current among both Christians and Mohammedans even at the present day :—" When the Turks took possession of Constantinople, a pious priest was saying Mass in Sancta Sophia. At the moment of the consecration the bearer of the evil tidings entered the church, and the priest prayed with great fervour, ' May God preserve the Holy Body of the Lord from profanation.' Suddenly the wall enclosed both Host and priest ; and (the belief is that) they will both re-appear unharmed on the day in which Constantinople shall be re-captured by the Christians." Even the story of the Seven Sleepers, in its literal and most miraculous sense, has been "defended and maintained with much learning by Assermani, a man of great literary reputation," as we are told by Pope Benedict XIV. in his "Treatise on Heroic Virtue" (Oratorian Translation, vol. iii., p. 244), a work which the reader may consult with advantage on the whole subject of ecstacies, natural and supernatural. "So I will have him to remain till I come, what is it to thee?" (John xxi. 22, 23.)

Note B. Page 39.

The subject of angelic operations in the powers of nature has been beautifully illustrated by F. Newman in a Sermon with which many readers will doubtless he well acquainted, and from which we make the following extract :—"What a number of beautiful and wonderful objects does Nature present on every side to us ! and how little we know concerning them ! In some indeed we see symptoms of intelligence, and we get to form some idea of what they are. For instance, about brute animals we know little, but still we see they have sense, and we understand that their bodily form which meets the eye is but the index, the outside token, of something we do not see. . . . But why do rivers flow ? Why does rain fall ? Why does the sun warm us ? And the wind, why does it blow ? Here our natural reason is at fault. . . . Reason tells us of no spirit abiding in what is commonly called the natural world, to make it perform its ordinary duties. Of course, it is God's will which sustains all ; so does God's will enable us to move also, yet this does not hinder but, in one sense, we may he truly said to move ourselves ; but how do the wind and water, earth and fire move ? Now here Scripture interposes, and seems to tell us that all this wonderful harmony is the work of Angels. Those events which we ascribe to chance, as the weather, or to nature, as the seasons, are duties done to that God who maketh His Angels to be winds, and His Ministers a flame of fire. For example, it was an Angel which gave to the pool at Bethesda its medicinal quality ; and there is no reason why we should doubt that other health-springs in this and other countries are made such by a like unseen ministry. The fires on Mount Sinai, the thunders and lightnings, were the work of Angels ; and in the Apocalypse we read of the Angels restraining the winds. Works of vengeance are likewise attributed to them. The fiery law of the volcanoes, which (as it appears) was the cause of Sodom and Gomorrah's ruin, was caused by the two Angels who rescued Lot. The hosts of Sennacherib were destroyed by an Angel, by means (it is supposed) of a suffocating wind. The pestilence in Israel, when David numbered the people, was the work of an Angel. The earthquake at the Resurrection was the work of an Angel. And in other parts of the Apocalypse the earth is smitten in various ways by Angels of vengeance.

"Thus, as far as the Scripture communications go, we learn that the course of Nature, which is so wonderful, so beautiful, and so fearful, is effected by the ministry of these unseen beings. Nature is not inanimate ; its daily toil is intelligent ; its works are duties. . . . As our souls move our bodies, be our bodies what they may, so there are Spiritual Intelligences which move those wonderful and vast portions of the natural world which seem to be inanimate ; and, as the gestures, speech, and expressive countenances of our friends around us enable us to hold intercourse with them, so in the motions of universal Nature, in the interchange of day and night, summer and winter, wind and storm, fulfilling His word, we are reminded of the blessed and dutiful Angels. . . . Whenever we look abroad, we are reminded of those most gracious and holy Beings, the servants of the Holiest, who deign to minister to the heirs of salvation. Every breath of air, and ray of light and heat, every beautiful prospect, is, as it were, the skirts of their garments, the waving of the robes of those whose faces see God in heaven."—Parochial Sermons, vol. ii., Sermon xxix.

Note C. Page 39.

Cornelius à Lapide thus comments on Gen. xxxii. 1, 2:—"Duas angelorum acies vidit hic Jacob ; inde enim hic locus Hebraice vocatus Machanaim, quod nomen est duale, et significat bina castra vel binas acies : unde et urbs ibidem postea ædificata dicta est Machanaim. Nimirum una acies erat angeli qui erat custos et præses Mesopotamæ : hic cum angelis sibi subditis et subordinatis, quasi instructa acie, comitatus fuerat, et secure deduxerat Jacobum a Mesopotamia hucusque, scilicet ad confinia Chananææ. Ibi occurrit ei eumque excepit angelus præses Chananææ cum sua acie angelorum sibi subditorum, ut eum per Chananæam secure ad patrem perduceret, et ab Esau aliisque ei infensis tueretur et protegeret."

Note D. Page 106.

Extract from B. Henry Suso's "Colloque Spirituel des Neuf Rochers :"—"Le Bienheureux vit le dernier rocher, qui était si élevé que l'œil pouvait à peine y atteindre . . . il en aperçut plusieurs qui faisaient leurs efforts pour y monter du huitième rocher, mais presque tous y renonçaient; deux ou trois seulement parvenaient à s'y fixer.

«Henri.—'Pourquoi, Seigneur, l'accès de ce rocher est-il si difficile ? Presque personne ne peut y arriver.'

"Jesus-Christ.—'Ce que est escarpé et élevé est nécessairement d'un accès difficile. Très-peu persévèrent jusqu'à la mort dans le détachement parfait d'eux-mêmes ; très-peu aussi parviennent à cette élévation. La plupart de ceux qui s'en approchent, en voyant la vie de ces saints si différente de celle des autres, si austère, si mortifiée, ont peur et retournent en arrière.'"—Œuvres du B. Henri Suso, p. 333.

Note E. Page 119.

In the Life of M. Olier, the Founder of the Seminary and Community of St Sulpice, we read that magic was systematically practised in his day, and that the Blessed Sacrament of the Altar was the object of the most horrible profanations. "Books on the diabolic art were publicly sold at the very doors of the church (of St Sulpice), and shortly after M. Olier entered on the duties of the parish, the bailie of the suburb, being in pursuit of three persons accused of sorcery, and mistaking one house for another, found an altar dedicated to the evil spirit, with these words inscribed upon it : Gratias tibi, Lucifer ; gratias tibi, Beelzebub ; gratias tibi, Azareel. The altar was a sort of travesty of that consecrated to Catholic worship ; the candles were black, the ornaments about it were all in keeping with its infernal object, and the book of prayers, as if in mockery of the Missal, consisted of diabolical incantations. The bailie took possession of the book, but the affair was not prosecuted any further on account of the numbers and position of those who were implicated."—Life of M. Olier, pp. 161, 162.

Note F. Page 121.

Mother Margaret, whose spirit was wonderfully akin to that of Boudon, often gives utterance to the same complaint. "' Pray, pray ! my dear children,' she writes from Longton, 'and be ready to make any sacrifice to save souls and advance God's Church on earth. See how little He makes Himself for ungrateful man!' . . . Actual poverty was not much felt in this population, and far more distressing to her heart than any temporal poverty endured by creatures was that to which she beheld our Divine Lord subjecting Himself within His own tabernacle. ' The wants of our God,' she writes, 'are far more visible here than those of His suffering members.' . . . She had not forgotten the chapel at Stoke, and was at this time begging for means to procure a silver ciborium for it. ' See how long, how patiently, the Eternal Wisdom waits,' she says, 'for His creatures to give Him a clean vessel in which to rest His Sacred Body, there to remain for the love of those who think it too much to give Him their left-off clothes.' . . . This was the poverty she loved best to relieve, the destitution whose appeals she could never resist. The language of her heart was ever that of David : ' Shall I dwell in a house of cedar, whilst the Lord dwelleth in curtains?' . . . We may say that it was her favourite charity to give to the Lord, and the subject of some of her most frequent exhortations to seculars. ' I fear,' she says in one of her letters from Longton, 'the rich will be rigorously judged at the last day for spending so much on their bodies, and leaving our Lord in poverty, rags, and dirt. Protestants may well doubt of the Presence of our Lord with us when we show so much coldness towards the place where His Majesty resides.' . . . .

"This continued sense of God, in which faith and love had an equal share, explains the ardour she always manifested in all that regarded His worship, and the profuse munificence with which she adorned His sanctuary. She would have lavished the wealth of an empire, had she possessed it, in the decoration of His temple and tabernacle. 'When our Mother had to provide anything for the Church,' said one of her earliest companions, 'it was as if she was ordering for some prince of boundless riches, to whom all the bills would be sent in.' This was undoubtedly her favourite devotion ; it far exceeded even her benevolence to the poor. She always impressed on her Religious that care for the service of God must come before charity to the poor, or the supply of their own necessities. ' It would be better that we should want bread,' she would say, ' than that our Lord should be neglected ; as to the poor, there are many to help them, but few people think of our hidden God.' . . . Nothing moved her so much as the least semblance of weariness and stinginess in what appertained to God's service ; whatever was given to Him was to be the best that could be given."—Life, pp. 211-13, 293-4.

THE END.

printed by balllantyne and company edinburgh and london

Now ready, cloth, 3s.

THE HIDDEN LIFE OF JESUS:

A Lesson and Model to Christians.

Translated from the French of
HENRI-MARIE BOUDON,
archdeacon of evreux.

by
EDWARD HEALY THOMPSON, M.A.

Lately published, cloth, 48.

THE LIFE OF M. OLIER,

Founder to the Seminary of St Sulpice;

WITH NOTICES

of
HIS MOST EMINENT CONTEMPORARIES.

by
EDWARD HEALY THOMPSON, M.A.

This Biography has received the special approbation of the Abbé Faillon, author of "La Vie de M. Olier," and of the Very Reverend Paul Dubreul, D.D., Superior of the Seminary of St Sulpice, Baltimore, U.S.

LIBRARY OF RELIGIOUS BIOGRAPHY.

EDITED BY

EDWARD HEALY THOMPSON, M.A.

Volumes already Published :—

I. The Life of ST ALOYSIUS GONZAGA, S.J. 5s.
II. The Life of MARIE-EUSTELLE HARPAIN, the Sempstress of Saint - Pallais, called "The Angel of the Eucharist." 5s.

To be ready at Christmas.

III. The Life of ST STANISLAS KOSTKA, S.J.

In Immediate Preparation :

IV. The Life of M. ORAIN, Parish Priest of Fegréac. This volume will be illustrated with details of the sufferings of the Breton Church during the "Reign of Terror."
V. The Life of V. MARIA CRISTINA of SAVOY, Queen of Naples.
VI. The Life of M. MARCEAU, Captain of the Missionary Ship L'Arche d'Alliance.

To be followed by Lives of

The Baron de Renty.
M. Boudon, Archdeacon of Evreux.
Armelle Nicolas, the Servant Girl of Campenéac.
Father de Condren, Superior of the French Oratory.
V. Anna Maria Taigi, the Roman Matron.
M. Gabriel de Vidaud, Model of Christians in the World.
V. Maria Clotilda of France, Queen of Sardinia.
Father Baptiste Muard, Founder of the Benedictine Preachers of the Sacred Hearts of Jesus and Mary.
Father Louis Lallemant and his Disciples.

Three Nirces of St Aloysius Gonzaga.
&c. &c. &c.

LONDON : BURNS & OATES, 17 AND 18 PORTMAN ST.

BURNS, OATES, & CO.'S LIST.

THE THREE MISSION BOOKS,
Comprising all that is required for general use ;
the cheapest books ever issued.

1. Complete Book of Devotions and Hymns : Path to Heaven, 1000 pages, 2s. This Volume forms the Cheapest and most Complete Book of Devotions for Public or Private use ever issued. (25th Thousand.) Cloth, Two Shillings. Also in various bindings.
2. *Complete Choir Manual (Latin) for the Year*, 230 pieces. 10s. *6d.*
3. *Complete Popular Hymn and Tune Book (English)*, 250 pieces. 10s. *6d.* Melodies alone, 1s. Words, *3d, ;* cloth, *5d.*

Prayers of St. Gertrude and Mechtilde. Neat cloth, lettered, 1s. 6d. ; Fr. morocco, red edges, 2s. ; best calf, red edges, 4s. ; best morocco, plain, 4s. 3d. ; gilt, 5s. 6d. Also in various extra bindings. On thin vellum paper at the same prices.

Devotions for the "Quaranf Ore," or New Visits to the Blessed Sacrament. Edited by Cardinal Wiseman. 1s., or in cloth, gilt edges, 2s. ; morocco, 5s.

Imitation of the Sacred Heart. By the Rev. Father Arnold, S.J. 12mo, 4s. 6d. ; or in handsome cloth, red edges, 5s. ; also in calf, 8s ; morocco, 9s.

Manual of the Sacred Heart. New edition, 2s.; red edges, 2s. 6d. ; calf, 5s. ; morocco, 5s. 6d.

The Spirit of St. Theresa. 2s. ; red edges, with picture, 2s. *6d.*

The Spirit of the Curé d'Ars. 2s. Ditto, ditto. 2s. 6d.

The Spirit of St. Gertrude. 2s. 6d.

Manna of the New Covenant ; Devotions for Communion. Cloth, 2s. ; bound, with red edges, 2s. 6d.

A"Kempis. The Following of Christ, in four books; a new translation, with borders, and illustrative engravings. Fcap. 8vo, cloth, 3s. 6d.; calf, 6s. 6d. ; morocoo, 8s. ; gilt, 10s. 3d. The same, pocket edition. Cloth, 1s. ; bound, roan, 1s. 3d. ; calf, 4s. ; morocco, 4s. 3d.

Spiritual Combat; a new translation. 18mo, cloth, 3s.; calf, 6s. ; morocco, 7s. The same, pocket size. Cloth, 1s. ; calf, neat, *4s.* ; morocco, 4s. 6d.

Burns, Oates, & Co., 63 Paternoster Row, E.C.

Missal. New and Complete Pocket Missal, in Latin and English, with all the new Offices and the Proper of Ireland, Scotland, and the Jesuits. Roan, embossed gilt edges, 4s. 6d. ; calf flexible, red edges, 7s. 6d. ; morocco, gilt edges, 8s. 6d. ; ditto, gilt, 10s.

Epistles and Gospels for the whole Year. 1s. 6d.

Vesper Book for the Laity. This Volume contains the Office of Vespers (including Compline and Benediction), complete for every day in the year. Roan, 3s. 6d. ; calf, 5s. 6d. ; morocco, 6s. 6d.

The Psalter in Latin, 1s. *3d. Do. in English :* new edition (*in the press*).

Easter in Heaven. By Father Weninger, S.J. 4s. 6*d.*

The Spirit of Christianity. From the French of Nepveu. 4s.

Considerations on the World. By Piot. 1s. 6*d.*

The Touchstone of Character. By the Abbé Chassay. 3s.

Crasset. Meditations for every Day in the Year. From the French of Père Crasset, S.J. 8vo, 8s.

Sancta Sophia. By Father Baker, O.S.B. 5s.

Lombez on Christian Joy. 1s. 9d.

Spirit of St. Francis of Sales. 8s. 6*d.*

Our Faith the Victory. By Dr. McGill. 10s.

Spiritual Maxims of St. Vincent de Paul. 1s. 4d.

The Art of Suffering. From the French of St. Germain. 1s. 6d.

Method of Meditation. By Father Roothan. 2s.

The Genius of Christianity. By Chateaubriand. Complete edition. 8*s.*

The Martyrs. By the same. 6s.

Hecker (Rev. J. T.). Aspirations of Nature. 5s.—Questions of the Soul. 4s. 6d.

Mission and Duties of Young Women. 2s. 6d.

Guide for Catholic Young Women. By Father Deshon. 4s.

Maynard on the Teaching of the Jesuits. 3s.

Mary, Star of the Sea. 3s. 3d.

Paradise of the Christian Soul. Complete. 6s.

The Words of Jesus. Edited by the Rev. F. Caswall. 1s.

Lyra liturgica : Verses for the Ecclesiastical Seasons. By Canon Oakeley. 3s. 6d.

Burns, Oates, & Co., 17 & 18 Portman Street, W.

Select Sacred Poetry. 1s.

Instructions in Christian Doctrine. 3s.

New Testament Narratine for Schools and Families. 2s. 6d.

Letters on First Communion. 1s.

Flowers of St. Francis of Assisi. 3s.

Manual of Practical Piety. By St. Francis de Sales. 3s. 6d.

Manresa; or the Spiritual Exercises of St. Ignatius. 3s.

The Christian Virtues. By St. Alphonsus. 4s.

Eternal Truths. By the same. 3s. 6d.

On the Passion. By the same. 3s.

Jesus hath loved us. By the same. 9d.

Reflections on Spiritual Subjects. By the same. 2s. 6d.

Glories of Mary. By the same. New edition. 3s. 6d.

The Raccolta of Indulgenced Prayers. 3s.

Rodriguez on Christian Perfection. Two vols. 6s.

Stolberg's Little Book of the Love of God. 2s.

The Treasure of Superiors. 3s. 6d.

Archbishop Hughes' Complete Works. Two vols. 8vo, 24s.

Sermons. By Father Baker. With Memoir. 8vo, 10s.

Devout Instructions on the Sundays and Holidays. By Goffine. 8vo, 9s. 6d.

Sermons by the Paulists of New York. First Series, 4s.; 2d ditto, 6s. ; 3d ditto, 5s. 6d. ; 4th ditto, 6s. ; 5th ditto (1865-6), 7s.

A Hundred Short Sermons. 8vo, 8s.

Spalding's (Bishop) Evidences. 7s.—Miscellanies. 12s. 6d.

The Gentle Sceptic. By Father Wallworth. A Treatise on the Authority and Truth of the Scriptures, and on the Questions of the Day as to Science, &c. 6s.

Family Devotions for every Day in the Week, with occasional Prayers. Selected from Catholic Manuals, ancient and modem. Foolscap, limp cloth, red edges, very neat, 2s.

Aids to Choirmasters in the Performance of Solemn Mass, Vespers, Compline, and the various Popular Services in General Use. 2d.

P.S. Messrs. B. & Co. will be happy to send any of the above Books on inspection.

A large allowance to the Clergy.

Burns, Oates, & Co., 63 Paternoster Row, E.C.

RELIGIOUS BIOGRAPHY AND HISTORY.

St. Aloysius Gonzaga. 5s.
St. Charles Borromeo. 3s. 6d.
St. Vincent de Paul. 3s.
St. Francis de Sales. 3s.
Marie Eustelle Harpam.
The Curé d'Ars. 4s.
St. Thomas of Canterbury. 4s. 6d.
Wyheham, Waynflete, & More. 4s.
The Blessed Henry Suso. 4s.
M. Olier of Saint Sulpice. 4s.
The Early Martyrs. 3s. 6d.
St. Dominic and the Dominican Order. 3s. 6d.
Madame Swetchine. 7s. 6d.
The Sainted Queens. 3s.
Blessed John Berchmans. 2s.
St. Brands Xavier. 2s.
St. Philip Neri. 3s.
St. Ignatius. 2s.
St. Brands of Rome. 2s.
Heroines of Charity. 2s. 6d.
Saints of the Working Classes. 1s. 4d.
Sœur Rosalie and Mdlle. Lamourons. 1s.
St. Francis and St. Clare. 1s.
Lives of Pious Youth. 3s. 6d.
Modem Missions in the East and West. 3s.
Missions in Japan and Paraguay. 3s.
Religious Orders, Sketches of. 4s. 6d.
The Knights of St. John. 3s. 6d.
Anecdotes and Incidents. 2s.
Remarkable Conversions. 2s. 6d.
Pictures of Christian Heroism. 3s.
Popular Church History. 3s.

Missions in India. 5s.

Lives of the Roman Pontiffs. By De Montor. Fine engravings. 2 very large vols. 58s. (cash, 50s.).

Darras' History of the Church. 4 vols. Edited by Bp. Spalding. Imperial 8vo. 2l. 8s. (cash, 2l.).

Butler's Lives of the Saints. 4 vols. cloth, 30s.

The Life of Bishop Borie. 2s.

The Life of Mary Ann of Jesus, the Lily of Quito. 3s. 6d.

Life of St. Ignatius. By Babtoli. 2 vols. 14s.

St. Ignatius and his Companions. 4s

The Life of Abulchar Bisciarah. 2 vols. 3s. 6d.

Life of Mme. de Soyecourt. 3s.

Life of St. Angela Merici. 3s. 6d.

Life of St. Margaret of Cortona. 3a 6d.

Life of Princess Borghese. 2s.

Life of F. Maria Ephraim. 5s. *Life of Mrs. Seton.* 8s. 6d.

Life of Mme. de la Peltrie. 2s.

Life of Father Felix de Andreis. 4s. 6d.

Life of St. Stanislaus. 1s. 6d.

Life of St. Philamena. 2s. 6d.

Life of St. Cecilia. By Gueranger. 6s.

Lives of Fathers of the Desert. 4s. 6d.

Life of Bishop Bruté. 3s. 6d.

Life of Pius VI. 3s.

Life of St. Bridget. 2s. 6d.

Life of St. Mary Magdalen. 2s. 6d.

Life of St. Zita. 3s.

Life of St. Brands of Assisi. 2s.

Life of St. Catherine of Sienna. 5s.

Life of Bishop Flaget. 4s. 6d.

Life of Dr. Maginn. 4s. 6d.

Life of Cath. M'Auley, Foundress of the Sisters of Mercy. 10s. 6d.

Shea (J. G.). Perils of the Ocean and Wilderness. 3s. 3d.

Shea (J. G.). Missions in the United States. 9s

Shea (J. G.). History of the Church in America. 7s. 6d.
Indian Sketches. By De Smet. 2s. 6d.
History of the Society of Jesus. By Daurignac. 2 vols. 12s. 6d.

Burns, Oates, & Co., 17 & 18 Portman Street, W.